ASIAN-EUROPEAN PERSPECTIVES

I0028171

Curzon-IIAS Asian Studies Series

Series Co-ordinator: Dick van der Meij
Institute Director: Wim A.L. Stokhof

The International Institute for Asian Studies (IIAS) is a postdoctoral research centre based in Leiden and Amsterdam, The Netherlands. Its main objective is to encourage Asian Studies in the Humanities and the Social Sciences and to promote national and international co-operation in these fields. The Institute was established in 1993 on the initiative of the Royal Netherlands Academy of Arts and Sciences, Leiden University, Universiteit van Amsterdam and Vrije Universiteit Amsterdam. It is mainly financed by The Netherlands Ministry of Education, Culture, and Sciences. IIAS has played an active role in co-ordinating and disseminating information on Asian Studies throughout the world. The Institute acts as an international mediator, bringing together various entities for the enhancement of Asian Studies both within and outside the Netherlands. The Curzon-IIAS Asian Studies series reflects the scope of the Institute. The Editorial Board consists of Erik Zürcher, Wang Gungwu, Om Prakash, Dru Gladney, Amiya K. Bagchi, James C. Scott, Jean-Luc Domenach and Frits Staal.

ASIAN-EUROPEAN PERSPECTIVES

DEVELOPING THE ASEM PROCESS

EDITED BY

Wim Stokhof
and
Paul van der Velde

Routledge
Taylor & Francis Group

LONDON AND NEW YORK

First Published in 2001
by Curzon Press

Published 2013 by Routledge

2 Park Square, Milton Park, Abingdon, Oxfordshire OX14 4RN
711 Third Avenue, New York, NY 10017

First issued in paperback 2014

Routledge is an imprint of the Taylor & Francis Group, an informa business

Editorial Matter © 2001 Wim Stokhof and Paul van der Velde

Typeset in Times New Roman by Dick van der Meij

All rights reserved. No part of this book may be reprinted or reproduced or utilised in
any form or by any electronic, mechanical, or other means, now known or hereafter
invented, including photocopying and recording, or in any information storage or
retrieval system, without permission in writing from the publishers.

British Library Cataloguing in Publication Data
A catalogue record of this book is available from the British Library

ISBN 978-0-700-71435-3 (hbk)
ISBN 978-1-138-86334-7 (pbk)

ACKNOWLEDGEMENTS

This publication would not have been possible without the enthusiastic co-operation and support of Wilton Park, Steyning (UK) on whose premises at Wiston House the conference 'Managing the Global Economy in the Light of the Asian Crisis which took place from 22 to 25 March 1999 was held. In particular we would like to thank the Chief Executive Director of Wilton Park, Colin Jennings, and the Associate Director of Wilton Park, Robin Hart. The majority of the contributions to this represent reworked versions of lectures held during the conference. We wish to thank all contributors to this publication for their patience and insightful articles.

Furthermore, we would like to express our gratitude to Dick van der Meij MA, whose aid in copy-editing was indispensable, and to Rosemary Robson FRAS BA (Hons.) for her English corrections on most parts of this publication.

The Editors

FOREWORD

This publication, *Asian-European Perspectives: Developing the ASEM Process*, is largely based on reworked versions of lectures held at the Wilton Park Conference 'Managing the Global Economy in the Light of the Asian Crisis', which took place from 22 to 25 March 1999. Some fifty specialists attended the conference from Asia and Europe who freely exchanged their views on the emerging new Europe-Asia relationship.

This book contains twelve contributions, ten of which are slightly edited versions of lectures held during the conference. In order to obtain a more complete picture of the ASEM process we asked Leo Schmit and Jürgen Rüland to write articles on the ASEM process from a sociological and politicological point of view respectively.

We have also added the Chairman's Statement at ASEM 3 (which was held in Seoul, 20-21 October 2000); the Asia-Europe Co-operation Framework 2000; and a summing up of activities since ASEM 2. The readers will notice that in the articles the future tense is used when referring to ASEM 3. We decided not to change this because the articles were indeed written prior to that meeting.

We hope that this publication as well as our first publication on this topic *ASEM The Asia-Europe Meeting. A Window of Opportunity* (London 1999) may serve as a small contribution towards encouraging the promising dialogue between Asia and Europe, not only in the ASEM framework but in other domains of society as well.

Wim Stokhof and Paul van der Velde

TABLE OF CONTENTS

ASIAN-EUROPEAN PERSPECTIVES

WIM STOKHOF AND PAUL VAN DER VELDE

The Asia-Europe Meeting (ASEM) was officially established in 1996 at the first summit in Bangkok. ASEM is an interregional forum which consists of seven members of the Association of Southeast Asian Nations (ASEAN), China, Japan, South Korea and the fifteen members of the European Union (EU). The main components of the ASEM process, which has so far been only loosely organized, include political dialogue, education and culture, security and the economy. In general, the process is considered by the parties involved to be a way of enhancing relations between Asia and Europe at all levels, a move which is deemed necessary to achieve a more balanced political, economic, and cultural world.

Now at the beginning of a new millennium there seems to be all the more reason to deepen this process because the US is downscaling its involvement world-wide. In Europe we are seeing a host of new developments emerging. The monetary Union has finally been established after many years of debate. Unfortunately a political union which would make the EU more resolute still seems far away, although there is a continuous political consultation on foreign policy between the most important countries in Europe. In the field of security a European Rapid Deployment Force is in the making. Additionally, some people do not realize that Europe is also a nuclear power. In the field of education the Declaration of Bologna will go a long way towards the uniformization of the curricula of higher education by the year 2010. The development of an accreditation system for higher education is an unequivocal sign that Europe is striving towards integration. The Convention of Nice which gave the official go-ahead to the further expansion of the EU is creating its own dynamism. In Asia there have also been numerous initiatives towards achieving a further integration.

This book, *Asian-European Perspectives: Developing the ASEM Process*, is a sequel to the book which we edited two years ago: *ASEM A Window of Opportunity* (London 1999). In that volume we took a look at the politicians' view of ASEM, the possibilities to improve mutual contact between Asia and Europe simultaneously trying to delineate the challenges and problem areas and hence map out the future of ASEM. In this volume the contributors will try to answer questions of a more practical nature or present views on the process, such as: the ideas the ASEM Vision Group has developed. How can the ASEM potential be realized? How can we create an usable ASEM vocabulary? How can we create a Eurasian Research culture? The answers to these questions are of paramount importance to the continuation of the process.

The contributions to this book are written by Asian and European academics, politicians, and businessmen. Most of them have been involved in ASEM from its inception and freely support the necessity of the process. This does not mean that they are not critical. On the contrary, many express strong doubts about the feasibility and durability of the ASEM process, but at the same time are conscious of the fact that without it the world will be a far less stable place in which to live. We, and all the contributors too, are involved in the ASEM process because we are convinced that if it had not been invented, it should have been invented. It is timely because the 'triangular world' - of which we saw the glimmerings a couple of years ago - is fast growing into a reality which we have to grasp before it is too late.

THE VISION GROUP'S VISION

The first three contributions to this volume are written by persons closely connected with the ASEM Vision Group which drew up a report entitled, *For a Better Tomorrow. Asia-Europe Partnership in the 21st Century* which can be considered the guidebook to ASEM for the next twenty-five years. Niels Helvig Petersen, Minister of Foreign Affairs of Denmark, a country which will host ASEM in 2002, in his article 'ASEM: Realising the Potential for the Next Millennium' strikes a positive note, although he is not blind to the shortcomings of the ASEM process. He is of the opinion that ASEM should serve as a facilitator and a bridge builder in creating a deeper understanding between Europe and Asia concerning some of the key issues which are on the global agenda. Therefore ASEM should gradually integrate Asia and Europe into an area of peace and shared development. In that context both regions should broaden their concepts of security and build regionally based crisis management capabilities. This broadening clearly anticipates a partial US military withdrawal from both the Asian and European theatres.

The title of the article by John Boyd, 'Being Serious about Asia', sounds like an overt warning to all Europeans who have not yet grasped the importance of Asia for Europe. He openly warns the countries of Europe that they cannot afford to ignore Asia whatever 'distractions' such as the enlargement of the EU or the introduction of the Euro there might be. At the same time he calls upon individuals to boost the process. Being a man with a wealth of Asia experience, Boyd knows that long-term personal relationships will not only give more substance and flavour to the process, but at the same time they will bolster the institutional framework of ASEM. In his argumentation, he pleads for the reinforcement of cultural contact and more transparency through the establishment of an international degree accreditation system and he favours benchmarking between the two regions. He thinks that this will serve to shed more light on testing systems and will also result in the use of 'best practices'. This could be one of the most promising outcomes of the ASEM process as a whole.

Robert S. Arendal who is a declared representative of the business community and a member of the Vision Group voices the private sectors' point of view most clearly. In his article, which bears the same title as the Vision Groups' report, he makes a strong plea for a multilateral trading system, a free flow of goods by 2025, and such meaningful initiatives as the Asia-Europe Trade Week. He is convinced that the ASEM process has to move beyond government circles and therefore needs strong inputs by businessmen and academics. Whereas in the beginning the ASEM process was first and foremost seen by politicians as a way to increase and develop economic co-operation, Arendal expresses some disappointment at the meagre concrete results which have been achieved in this domain so far.

REALIZING ASEM'S POTENTIAL

In his article 'Resolving the Paradox' Anthony Murphy points out the paradox underlying the relationship between the private sector and the government in the ASEM process. Some see this relationship as its greatest strength while others conceive of it as its most serious weakness. The paradox should be resolved otherwise ASEM, as a process in which the private sector has an active role, will lose its credibility. Among the reasons ASEM might have to cede this credibility in the eyes of the business community is the lack of such crucial factors as focus, engagement, continuity, and feedback. Quick results serve to get by on but they rarely endure or have a long-lasting impact. Therefore, ASEM business forums should learn from other similar forums such as the Transatlantic Business Dialogues (TABD) and the APEC Business Advisory Council (ABAC) in order to increase their own bargaining power.

In his contribution 'The ASEM Process: New Rules for Engagement in a Global Environment' Leo Schmit takes a bird's eye view on the sociological and historical development of the process during the first five years of its existence. He refers to Prime Minister Goh Chok Tong of Singapore, who stated that there are three stages the ASEM process will have to go through before it reaches a mature status: getting to know each other, constructive dialogue, and consensus-based policy making. Schmit feels that we have moved into the second stage. He sees a clear role for Europe in Asia when it comes down to balancing US influence in the area, which would set the stage for a more stable world. In view of the fact that the EU is the biggest lender to and investor in Asia, the Euro has the potential to become more widely used in international transactions and may help to prevent a *de facto* inclusion of Asian countries in the Dollar zone. The EU has other important advantages over the US as it has a more highly developed capacity for inter-governmental co-operation and for the building up of regional institutes across natural borders, which are highly relevant to Asia where regional diversity is also a matter of course.

In his article 'Does ASEM function as a transregional Forum?', Jürgen Rüland gives us the global setting of the ASEM process and the way he perceives its development. Whereas after World War II he identifies the foundation of global organisations such the UN, in the fifties these seemed to give way to regional organizations such as the EU, which were primarily established to create an own identity. However, these lost weight again in the sixties and seventies. At the end of the eighties they again began to gain strength. Rüland labels this second wave the open regionalism in which is the regional organizations become complementary to the global organizations. Regional co-operation is now a chance for building up more bargaining power in international forums.

As a transregional forum ASEM could assume an intermediary role between the regional and the global policy levels, but to do this ASEM must become more result-oriented. In turn this would require the institutionalization of ASEM as an organization. Rüland argues that the Europe-Asia identity building has already gone much further at an informal level than at a governmental level. He is specifically referring to the work done by NGOs on sensitive issues which have not been tackled at the governmental level such as human rights, democracy, and child labour. This remark gives the next contribution of Kiyoko Ikegami an extra dimension.

INVENTING AN ASEM VOCABULARY

In her contribution 'Legal Status of Non-Profit Organizations in Japan' Ikegami gives an insightful example of Japanese lawmaking while at the same time demonstrating how the meaning of a concept such as NGO can differ completely from one context to the other. Ikegami zooms in on the increasingly important role NGOs play in present-day Japan. She refers to the earthquake in Kobe in 1995 where volunteers rushed in to do the job the paralysed government bureaucracy was incapable of undertaking. Thus the

NGOs were clearly pushed into the public realm because the government could not produce an effective response. The upshot was the emergence of a debate on the position of NGOs, organizations which up to that point in time had had a very feeble legal basis and therefore were hampered in their development. Ikegami states that it was the first time the citizens won a role in political decision making. The NPO Act was passed in 1998 as a consequence of negotiations between the citizens' organizations and the legislature. She sees this as a positive development which carries the potential of giving an increased Japanese grassroots level input to ASEM. The present-day Japanese NGOs are now more readily comparable to their ASEM counterparts or branches in Europe.

In his contribution 'How to Facilitate Integration of Developing Nations into the ASEM Process', Ngyuen Son views ASEM primarily as a co-operation based on mutual benefits with preferential policies from developed countries to support resource-development programmes in the developing countries. These countries in turn are doing their utmost to abolish any obstacles which stand in the way of a multilateral trade system and a free flow of capital, goods, and services. Despite this positive note, he sounds a warning stating that trade-development thinking should move beyond ideas of pure trade growth to include the enhanced participation of all nations in international trade, the reduction of the inequality between rich and poor nations, and an improved quality of life for all. He hopes that these high-set goals can be achieved by the improvement of technological and scientific co-operation.

Daljit Singh addresses another increasingly important topic in his article 'Europe and Asia: Promoting Security and Political Co-operation'. He makes a plea for more European involvement in Asia, because he considers Europe (after two world wars) in contrast to Asia to provide a relatively peaceful environment. The investments in security should be brought more in balance with the major European investments in the Asian economy. Europe should strive primarily to transfer its knowledge and experience in the fields of preventive diplomacy, confidence building, and peace keeping. This would be specifically useful in potential, or actual, areas of conflict in Asia such as the South China Sea, the Taiwan Straits, and the Korean Peninsula. Singh believes the Asians would welcome this because at this point in history Europe does not have any interest in dominating any part of Asia. Europe could also be of assistance in facilitating the rise of China as a peaceful player in the global area.

CREATING A EURASIAN RESEARCH CULTURE

In her contribution, 'ASEM: Time for an Overhaul', Nuria Ofken tries to find an answer to the question of what has been achieved by ASEM. And to that of what direction it should take. She examines the main components of ASEM, political dialogue, economic co-operation, and cultural exchange to find out whether progress has been made in these fields in fostering a closer relationship between the two regions, something she considers to be the fundamental goal of the process. In the fields of political dialogue and economic co-operation she sees little progress being made and quotes the failed attempts to advance customs' co-operation and investment facilitation, and that no common position could be arrived at on the necessary reform of the UN, as examples. She is more optimistic about cultural rapprochement between the two regions pointing out the activities of the Asia-Europe Foundation (ASEF). Notwithstanding small successes in the field of cultural exchange she pleads for a clear-cut ASEM agenda because only in this manner will ASEM fulfil its objective of initiating and sustaining collective learning processes, and thereby contributing to mutual understanding between the two regions.

In their contribution, 'The Need for an ASEM Research Platform', Sabine Kuypers and Wim Stokhof give high priority to education and research. Although treated in an off-hand manner over the past few years, they could now re-emerge as prime favourites because of the slow progress made in developing the economic, political, and security pillars of ASEM. Many contributors to this book are inclined to adopt the point of view that deepening the relationship and solidifying the foundation of the process are essential but remain largely unknown, because the results are not immediately visible. Given that politicians are very result-oriented, academics should play a more important role in the process in order to make it more balanced. Petersen underlines this point of view by pleading for the setting up of a focal point to facilitate twinning arrangements and other forms of institutional co-operation between universities and technical colleges in Asia and Europe. Could this be the ASEM Research Platform Kuypers and Stokhof are pleading for? ASEM is not only about the exchange of elements of civilizations, but also about the creation of a new civilization: the Eurasian which will co-exist alongside other great civilizations.

In the last contribution to this volume by César de Prado Yepes, entitled 'Towards a Virtual ASEM: From Information to Knowledge', the author accentuates the role new technology can play in boosting the ASEM process. He quotes President Kim Dae-Jung of Korea who made a strong plea for a Trans-Eurasian e-Network. This Network would not come as a bolt from the blue sky because there is an intensive co-operation between Asian and European multinationals in developing standards for GSM and UMTS. Although English is the language used most on the Internet, joint Asian and European efforts have paved the way for a multilingual Internet by developing software for characters. De Prado Yepes hopes that the Asian-Europe co-operation in the electronic field will stimulate the creation of virtual cultural and educational spaces even more. He is also aware that the convergence of existing structures at university and research level will be greatly enhanced by benchmarking and the development of an accreditation system which will create the critical mass the ASEM needs in order to achieve its goals.

MOBILIZING THE COPENHAGEN SENSES

One could arrive at the conclusion that ASEM has lost its momentum. But appearances deceive. Because the process was first and foremost perceived as a way to increase economic co-operation, the 'Asian crisis' of 1998 intruded itself as an annoying spoil-sport.

At a political level ASEM has not yet been able to formulate real common views leaving aside more rhetorical agreement on such hot issues as sexual abuse and so forth. Security has played a very limited role in the process but has become somewhat more important now that the US is scaling down its world-wide operations.

In the meantime the cultural pillar, which received least attention from the politicians, has done what it could with the meagre funds allocated to it. The foundation of ASEF gave the cultural co-operation an institutional basis from which to operate and produce results which it did. Therefore the majority of the contributors to this book, who represent all the layers of the process come more or less to the conclusion that for the time being culture is the way ahead for ASEM. Thanks to the activities of ASEF and other informal initiatives, for instance at NGO level, great progress in *lasting* co-operation has been made, not least because these organizations made it possible to deal with sensitive issues which lie at the heart of ASEM such as labour relations and human rights. These have to be solved first before many other aspects of ASEM can be treated in a meaningful manner.

The vast majority of the populations of the Asian and European countries are not aware of the process as such and therefore they are also ignorant of the importance of the intensification of the Eurasian relationship. This low degree of popular participation is reflected in the virtual absence of interest shown in ASEM by the press. When Number 3 was held in Seoul, the main newspapers passed over it in virtual silence. In our previous volume we remarked that ASEM should be for the people or it would not survive. We abide by this remark and propose that alongside the intensification of exchange programmes for students, high-school pupils, popular sitcoms with a mixed Eurasian cast addressing problems of day to day life in both areas should also be developed. These would contribute enormously to the sensitization of the populations of the ASEM countries. Europeans could come to the conclusion that the Asianization of Europe has advanced much further than they could ever have imagined, while Asians could see the Europeanization in a completely different perspective. If we are talking about the exchange of elements of civilizations, we should open ourselves to it. Asian-European Perspectives are everywhere. One only has to develop one's senses to see, hear, feel, and enjoy them. ASEM 4 in Copenhagen should become synonymous with the mobilization of the EURASIAN senses!

THE VISION GROUP'S VISION

CHAPTER 1

ASEM: REALISING THE POTENTIAL FOR THE NEXT MILLENNIUM

NIELS HELVIG PETERSEN

The sweeping changes in international affairs in the post-Cold War era have not left European-Asian relations untouched. Asia and Europe already share a long history in trade, culture, and politics. The collapse of the old bipolar world order has paved the way for Europeans and Asians to diversify and intensify relations across old barriers. Most importantly, it has resulted in growing awareness that a stronger European-Asian partnership will be key to confronting the economic, social, environmental, and security-related challenges of the new millennium.

THE IDEA AND HOW FAR WE HAVE COME

Asia and Europe constitute two of the world's most influential regions by any standard. More than two-thirds of the world's population lives in Asia and Europe. Despite the recent financial crisis, Asia is set to experience faster economic growth than any other region as the new century unfolds. Europe, for its part, is bolstering its own potential for growth through the European Monetary Union and the impending process of enlargement of the Union with the addition of new Member States from Central and Eastern Europe. At the political level both Europe and Asia are in the process of shaping their own regional identity in line with their specific historical circumstances.

In spite of this, European-Asian relations remain underdeveloped and underutilized compared to relations between America and Europe and America and Asia. By launching the Asia-European Meetings (ASEM), Heads of State and Government from Europe and Asia resolved at their Summit in Bangkok in 1996 to rectify this imbalance by establishing a framework for the development of a comprehensive Asian-European partnership.

Since the very beginning Denmark has been a staunch supporter of the ASEM-process. In a period of rapid international change we believe Europeans and Asians have much to gain by sharing their rich and varied experience and by discussing approaches and possible solutions to the issues confronting them. The flexible and broad-based nature of the ASEM process covering political, economic, and cultural issues makes it particularly well suited to the purpose. As a token of our commitment to the process, Denmark has offered to host the bi-annual ASEM Summit of Heads of State and Government in 2002.

Since the inaugural meeting in Bangkok, the ASEM process has made a good start. Both in Bangkok and at the subsequent London Summit, the Heads of State and Government provided clear guidance and direction to the future course of the process. Indeed the strong political leadership exerted at the summits and at the ministerial meetings in between continues to be one of the hallmarks of the process and one of the main reasons for its success. The broad spectrum of subjects covered ensures that the process offers something of interest to all ASEM Member States. The last four years have witnessed a growing number of ASEM-related activities in almost all areas of co-operation. This certainly testifies to the vibrancy of the process, but also makes it more difficult to develop a clear-cut ASEM profile.

The idea is not that ASEM should develop into a miniature UN or in other ways duplicate the work and discussions taking place in other specialized international forums. Instead, ASEM should serve as a facilitator and a bridge-builder in creating a deeper understanding between Europe and Asia concerning some of the key issues on the global agenda.

MAJOR CHALLENGES AHEAD

In order to ensure the continued relevance of the process in the twenty-first century, ASEM must be seen to address the main challenges facing Asia and Europe and to make a contribution to the debate on how to meet them. With this in mind the London Summit in 1998 decided to establish an Asia-Europe Vision Group (AEVG) to develop a medium- to long-term vision to help guide the future direction of the ASEM process. The group, comprising independent experts from the member states, has recently submitted a most interesting and thoughtful report. The report is guided by the overall vision of gradually integrating Asia and Europe into an area of peace and shared development and it contains a large number of specific proposals to this end. The Vision Group Report will be an important contribution to the deliberations on the future course of the ASEM process at the Summit in Seoul. The challenges facing us are indeed numerous and complex. They embrace economic, environmental, social, political, and security-related problems – some shared, others very different. I will address a few which I should be on the ASEM agenda in the years ahead.

4

POLITICAL AND SECURITY MATTERS

The informal dialogue on political developments in the regions of mutual interest and concern remains one of the main pillars of the ASEM-process. Although ASEM is not and should not be a forum for resolution of specific disputes and conflicts, the political dialogue serves an important purpose in clarifying positions and building confidence both within and between the two regions.

In spite of significantly reduced global military tension, the post-Cold War era has turned out to be less peaceful than we expected. Military threats of the past both in Asia and Europe have been replaced by more diffuse threats to peace and stability. They cover a broader spectrum of challenges to the economic, social, political, and environmental fabric of societies. As a result, the concept of security has become wider and our own security has become more intertwined with that of other regions. Whereas previously power and influence were determined by and large by the size of a country's military forces and economy, factors such as diplomacy, trade and good governance have become important elements in the concept of security. This broader view also attributes added weight to crisis management, preventive diplomacy, and conflict resolution

In Europe, we have just now begun the process of adjusting to the new and broader concept of security and its implications. A new European security architecture is in its formative stages. Former members of the Warsaw Pact are becoming members of NATO. The Kosovo crisis has demonstrated the need to strengthen European crisis management, *inter alia* through closer co-operation between the EU and NATO and by strengthening the Organisation of Security and Cooperation in Europe (OSCE).

Asia seems to be facing many of the same challenges in adapting to the new security environment, but in Asia the regional co-operative arrangements in the field of security are less elaborate. The recent crisis in East Timor clearly demonstrated the need for a regionally based crisis management capability.

In the years to come ASEM could play an important role as a catalyst for increased exchange of information and experience between Europe and Asia on adjusting to the new security environment. ASEM could be instrumental in facilitating greater co-operation between OSCE and Asian security institutions, such as the ASEAN Regional Forum, on confidence-building measures (CBMs), early warning systems, preventive diplomacy and so forth. Similarly, ASEM should encourage and facilitate increased co-operation and net-working between private research institutions, universities, NGOs and other civil society organizations on issues such as conflict prevention, civil-military relations and the like. Finally, we should also look at possibilities for enhanced co-operation on peacekeeping training and capacity building, particularly on the increasingly complex interface between military and civilian components of such operations.

PEOPLE-TO-PEOPLE CONTACTS AND THE HUMANE SOCIETY

We must not forget that the ultimate beneficiaries of the ASEM process should be the citizens of Europe and Asia. Ways should be explored to bolster people-to-people co-operation in ASEM, particularly within the educational and research sectors. Seminars, workshops, exchange programmes for students and scholars, and multilateral research programmes are already taking place, but their numbers and scope could be significantly increased. ASEM could, for example, consider setting up a focal point to facilitate twinning arrangements and other forms of institutional co-operation between universities and technical colleges in Europe and Asia.

Other ways of opening up ASEM to the public and increasing its relevance should also be explored. The creation of a permanent ASEM web-site as a point of reference for news and information on current issues related to the process could be a modest beginning. However, we should resist the inclination to steer or control initiatives, but should instead take a demand-driven approach and let the public avail itself of the new opportunities as it pleases.

Globalization of the world economy is bound to intensify in the twenty-first century. In an inexorably more globalized world national economies will face difficulty fostering social and economic development if they rely excessively on domestic resources. At the same time it has become evident that the globalization process is a complex and contrasting phenomenon. On the one hand it knits countries closer together than ever before in a global village through expanding international markets and modern information technology. On the other hand the globalization process amplifies and sometimes aggravates existing inequalities in the distribution of wealth and resources among and inside states. The recent Asian financial crisis demonstrated in a dramatic way the vulnerability of Asian economies and particularly the fragility of social progress to sudden, external financial shocks.

The process of globalization raises a host of issues. At the national level one must consider the extent to which the state should intervene to correct market imperfections. Related issues involve the role of good governance, the need to manage social imbalances and the imperative of preventing inequalities in income, access to education and the like to raise to levels where they pose a threat to social cohesion.

In early 1999 Denmark and the Republic of Korea jointly hosted an ASEM conference on States and Markets in Copenhagen with a view to promoting a common understanding of some of the key policy challenges facing European and Asian countries on economic and social progress in an increasingly globalized world. The discussions revealed a strong interest among ASEM Members in exchanging experience, and tapping the best practices and policy options in this field. The conference helped place the question of social progress squarely on the ASEM agenda and will no doubt give rise to new initiatives aimed at taking the discussions on these issues forward.

ECONOMIC AND TRADE POLICY CO-OPERATION

The economic and trade policy co-operation structures constitute a main pillar in ASEM. A major achievement at the London Summit was the Trade Pledge to refrain from raising tariffs in response to the Asian crisis. The Trade Pledge helped curb the negative effects of the economic and financial crisis and kept protectionism at bay.

The break down of the third ministerial conference of the WTO clearly demonstrates how important strong trade policy co-operation between the two regions will be also in the future. ASEM has the potential to become an essential bridge-builder when looking forward towards the launch of the coming round of trade negotiations that unfortunately could not be initiated in Seattle.

Another milestone at the London summit was the establishment of an ASEM Trust Fund under the auspices of the World Bank and the European Financial Expertise (EFEX) network of services within the European Commission, aimed at providing advice and technical assistance to the countries affected by the financial crisis.

The main scope of the ongoing economic co-operation within ASEM is to improve the climate for doing business between the two regions eventually creating jobs and enhancing standards of living in both regions. The Trade facilitation Action Plan (TFAP), the investment promotion Action Plan (TFAP), and the Asia Europe Business Forum (AEBF) are central to this end and close contacts have been established at both a high political level and at the level of government officials, experts and business-people for implementation.

But we need to go even further. In the years ahead we should work towards the target of free trade among ASEM partners in tandem with the efforts to ensure free trade at a global level. Liberalization of trade and capital flows call for the establishment of a new global financial architecture. While this new architecture should be agreed upon at international level, ASEM could play an important bridge-building role in bringing the discussions forward.

Co-operation on economic issues should continue to be an important element of ASEM. ASEM should endeavour both to strengthen trade and investment ties between the EU and Asia and to help shape alliances between Europe and Asia on key issues confronting the WTO and other multilateral economic fora.

THE ROAD TO COPENHAGEN

ASEM has got off to a good start. Its potential for dialogue and co-operation is far from exhausted. The ASEM process is more necessary than ever before. Denmark will continue to assign high priority to ASEM as a framework for the formation of a strong Asian-European partnership. The offer to host the ASEM 4 Summit in the second half of 2002 testifies to our determination to see the process move forward and to make a substantive contribution towards shaping the future agenda of ASEM.

CHAPTER 2

BEING SERIOUS ABOUT ASIA

JOHN BOYD

I have one message: it is essential to be serious about Asia. The Asia-Europe Vision Group has worked in this spirit, and I commend our Report. I do not claim that it is perfect but I do claim the importance of the effort and the signal it gives. The advantages of a strong relationship with Asia are clear, the costs of neglect equally so. But we all need reminding. Other things are competing for the attention of Europe - continuing pressures in the Balkans, the challenges of enlargement and institutional reform, daily issues of security, environment, currency and growth. The Asian economies are much better than they were but are not permanently out of the woods. Growth in Europe is hampered by its structures, and its economy offers pale competition to the energy and innovation of the US, growing at 4 per cent. Against this background the *Times* newspaper has rightly warned us in Europe against a retreat into provincial focus and, worse, loss of the post-war habit of viewing the human race as a whole. This would be a tragic reversal of our destiny.

In this article I want to address a series of specific questions. Do we have the focus on Asia right? Is there a mature European view? Is enough being done to follow up? Is there enough public information? Are we doing enough to inspire ordinary people? Have matters evolved since the Vision Group reported in April 1999 in a way that undercuts its conclusions?

In asking these questions I admit the usual risk of generalization and the difficulty of definition. Asia is not unitary, but vast and varied. Continuity impresses, but so does change, in many respects radically. Much of Asia is still responding in its own way to the challenge of the modern world.

I have not served everywhere in Asia, and there is in any case no such thing as an old hand. Nevertheless, with all allowances made, the central answer to my question - sufficient focus on Asia or not - must be 'Not quite'. There is much unrealized potential in the Europe-Asia relationship. And there is room for development of conscious partnership on the model of, for instance, the strong UK effort in Japan. Europe cannot afford to ignore Asia, whatever the current distractions.

REALIZING THE POTENTIAL

Let me start at individual level. Asia calls for a strong personal investment by Europeans, not least in language study. My own East Asian service happens to have taken me at one time or another to China, Hong Kong and Japan. I have increasingly visited Korea, particularly in the Vision Group process. Work or personal curiosity has taken me to Mongolia and the greater part of the South East Asia. Burma too is on my map. None of these are remotely remarkable for young Europeans these days. Many students, school children too, expect their campus to be involved in Asia whether through recruitment, exchanges, image projection, or the pursuit of funds. I attach particular importance myself to science and technology co-operation between my University and Asia. But the links require effort, objectivity, and financial back-up.

On the plus side, European economic investment in Asia remains for-midable. The pamphlet 'Societies in Transition' (1998) brought this out, EU external trade with East Asia representing at the time 25 per cent of the EU total, not that far behind US trade; and EU direct investment in East Asia 26 per cent of the total, with the UK on 14 per cent. The pamphlet showed European banks dwarfing most others in lending to the region. The link is multiple and complex, ranging from banking and business co-operation to development aid projects. Many Europeans live, work, and prosper in Asia.

But what about the famous debate on values? Are we heading different ways over time? I think not. Human needs, technology, crisis management drive us to make common cause. Academics underline differing time scales - the length of history and memory in Asia versus the relatively brief European engagement. Rightly so: Asia does, certainly, think of Europe in a special time frame - starting in 1500 and seen from the receiving end. But we owe it to ourselves to bring discussion back from colonialism to the pursuit of mutual advantage today. Asia and Europe are vitally important to each other and to the global balance. It is a commonplace that economic, political, and military events in Asia stand to affect Europe's own security and welfare. Less commented on is the reverse case, missed opportunity - potential close partners who fail to click through lack of imagination. The ASEM Vision Group paper is targeted precisely at a 'better tomorrow,' with strong inputs to global solutions by Europe and Asia alike.

If these assertions sound just that, let me try harder. As I say, my own experience has been practical. Diplomats are expected to get results and have to meet a timetable. They need to cope with today's demands, local reality, the style in which others operate, and their partners' own ambitions and perceptions. The present contributes to outcomes as much as the past.

Let us however try looking at the past as an asset. We Europeans have old relationships, in plural. There is much to build on. Wellington learnt in Bengal how to beat the French. All European states had a cultural and trading relationship with China. All were poised from the sixteenth century off the south coast of China to take advantage of a stunning regional market, and the Portuguese in particular can take credit for the earliest introduction to China and then to Japan of modern defence technology.

Remember that the Europeans were for much of this time eating with their fingers. Still, Europe made its own cultural inputs. I have a particular affection for Father Adam Schall, the Jesuit, who arrived in 1622, enjoying special dispensation to teach Copernicus in China even if that was in principle forbidden by the Vatican. Schall too brought Western technology, including an arsenal for China, achieved social status (if not as high as he reported to base) and above all developed the ability to communicate exactly.

European thought, capital and skills were deeply involved in the post-Renaissance and post-Ming development of Asia. Later, in the steam age, Hong Kong formed a tremendous base for diversified Western inputs in a region where Scots did much of the banking, an Ulsterman developed the Maritime Customs, Americans and Scandinavians traded vigorously, Englishmen built ships, French were in the Red River and Germans in Shantung. In a fluid diplomatic environment there could be no permanent monopolies.

Many Europeans took part, similarly, in the birth of modern Japan, The Dutch introduced *Rangaku* or Western science to Japan which to a large degree facilitated the transition to a modern industrial state. The UK and France were as ever in striking competition. German medicine arrived in the 1870s, the contribution of Prussia to the constitution was made in the 1880s. Hegel was influential and then Marx. Russia loomed as a strategic fact.

Setting up in Asia required, as always, risk-taking and investment. European numbers were small, challenges large. At the time of the first steps one and half million Portuguese were, culturally speaking, taking on 20 million Japanese or 100 million Chinese. Britain's own first trading post in Japan, 1612, was no more than a foothold. There were casualties too. As late as the nineteenth century diplomats were attacked. The cemetery in Macao is the last resting-place of young merchant navy crewmen and missionaries of every hue. That at Yokohama salutes engineers who helped to build Japan's railways. The Europeans faced cultural, financial, and linguistic challenges (and I must pay tribute to the early interpreters). But no wonder they went East. Museums in Berlin, London, Paris, Stockholm, Vienna and elsewhere remind us of what we have acquired from Asia. There were gains to be made in every direction.

11

One appreciates all the more the rugged local defence of the Asian tradition. We in Europe have benefited from the quality and flow of invention from Asia over a much longer time scale than the converse - paper, printing, the mariner's compass, gunpowder, silk, porcelain, not to mention impressive modern industrial and management achievements. China and Korea have a great inventive history from flood control to urban organization. The English poets Milton and Gray refer admiringly to Asian achievements in transport and porcelain. Japanese ingenuity speaks for itself - from their own Nobel and Fields laureates to their sense of space. Item, Churchill College, Cambridge, clearly reflecting what followers of Frank Lloyd Wright absorbed from Japan.

TOWARDS A STRONG ASIA POLICY

But background is not a policy. Can we in the years ahead establish a more solid policy basis? That Europe needs a policy I have no doubt and a strong policy too. We need a long view and a constant one. There is no point my asserting that we 'need each other'. The needs must be analysed, demonstrated, and catalogued. We need to build popular support at both ends.

Public and private European attitudes have been particularly tested recently by the Asian financial crisis. Markets in Europe react quickly to change. There has been a temptation, just at the turn of the century, to write Asia out of the scenario. Portfolios and ratings remain heavily scrutinized. The capacity of Asia for structural reform has been questioned, often impatiently. Meanwhile, Asians themselves ask, are Europeans prepared to stick with a long-term bet on Asia? Part of our answer came in Berlin, at the 1999 meeting of ASEM Foreign Ministers. The EU Presidency made the important point that there are no such things as 'European mathematics' or 'Asian economics' these days. The host foreign minister commented robustly on the capability of Asia to survive and on the real progress of reforms there. This could equally be the British view I think. There was useful emphasis on the total character of the Asia-Europe relationship, covering not only trade and finance but governance and the environment.

I am not interested in writing a national tract but I will draw four lessons from UK experience. First, be in Asia early and remain there (we were part of the early development and profiling of China, Japan, and Korea). Two, ensure support for specialist institutions dealing with Asia. SOAS serves a European public. The new East Asia Institute in Cambridge helps to bring modern China into sharper focus. Three, aim for transparency and play to your natural strengths. The UK, for these very reasons, has attracted 40 per cent of Japanese investment in Europe and has drawn deeply on a tradition of naval engineering co-operation. And of course tea has seen my country round many a tight corner (the cargo weighed 2 lbs. in 1664, 30 million by the 1820s).

As a declaration of faith, Asia is permanently important to Europe. The issue is not just economic. We are talking about the exchange of civilizations, the sharing of skills, and the evolution of political and social character. It is an exchange. Assets to build on include technical imagination and established habits of mutual recognition and co-operation. Asia's economic retreat is temporary. On the ground there is a reform process. Further transparency will cure much. I think we in Europe see what we should support.

Let me develop these points in a little more detail. China is as always a central topic. How the rest of us relate to it to best mutual advantage seems always controversial, but social and political evolution is, to me, a fact. In policy, realism must be the watchword. Naturally diplomats are attacked for saying that, but experience highlights the need for patience - and an ability to bite one's lip. One's own side can be embarrassing too: some foreign teachers in China thought they saw the realization of early Christianity, in the first manifestations of the Chinese Cultural Revolution.

The situation of Chinese citizens is infinitely better than when I first served there. In the years following the Great Leap there was little to admire on the streets of China beyond continuing courtesy and a gritty ability to survive. The China I first saw was a thoroughgoing dictatorship, ideological and personal, with dire imposition of one man's ideas down to street level. Farmers were essentially tied to the soil. There was ruthless suppression of dissent, often by guile. The foreigner's life was marked by aggressive exhortation, travel restrictions, the shortage of goods, and a variety of intrusions. Maoism, however diluted by corruption, greed, and internal distance, did very little for China.

And it was truly a world apart. On the ground in those days, no Americans. No Japanese. No Canadians. No Australians. The French only recently. No West Germans. Very little interaction politically between our small European missions and China. A sense of void. I view subsequent change, which has continued throughout my working lifetime, against that background. It leaves me a strong admirer of Deng Xiaoping. The previous goal for all, set rigidly from the top, has given way substantially to individual instinct, rapid growth, social room to breathe, and acceptance of political risk in the interests of modernization. I have no doubt that China is, in aggregate, a much better place.

All will not run smoothly. Reform of the state sector is problematic. The leadership has to deal with corruption and well-known problems in the Party and the Police. Too much growth still relies on state inputs. The refusal to devalue deserves praise but carries its own risks. Liberty of the subject is still to play for. State policy could be aggressive off shore. There are continuing challenges therefore to Western partners.

Nevertheless it must surely be right to persist in building a new relationship with China. History does provide clues. The objective of Europe should be to contribute strongly to the wider integration of China, that is, encourage her to embrace a shared global agenda from open markets to environmental clean-up. As a moral compass the aim must be to see full realization of humane practices. The leverage is the interest of China in national economic advance and global stability. To maximize her stake in trade rules and modern ideas cannot be done by isolation. The potential of China's membership of the WTO will solve this problem.

Korea hosts ASEM 3. This is timely. Even now she is regaining vigour. Indeed her economy has rebounded remarkably. That is not surprising in this tough and resourceful society. Structural change will, I am sure continue. The president is committed to positive change and active diplomacy. Europe needs a stable, yet evolving Korean Peninsula, just as Asia needs it. Diplomatic efforts to defuse problems there must be sustained. The course of events on that distant ground impacts importantly on Europe, hence a certain UK lead on the Korean Peninsula Economic Development Organization (KEDO). Appointees from EU member states worked notably well with their Korean counterparts on the Vision Group Report. Korea can take justifiable pride in the document.

The huge problems facing Japan are recognized - the recognition may be overdone. The collapse of the Japanese bubble has been well publicized, and the domestic mood remains unconfident. One keeps an open mind on whether the worst is really past. This should not fill Europeans with the remotest joy. Our interest is clear - in seeing Japan more self-confident. She is a great and proven partner for Europe. She needs us to balance a relationship with the US that can, viewed from Tokyo, seem overwhelming. We need Japan to pick up vigorously the burdens of global stabilization and relief of need. In trade policy each needs the other. In the last few years Japan has moved steadily (if slowly) in the liberal direction. This must be to our mutual interest. Jointly we can reinforce (or if we are clumsy, undermine) the liberal instinct in North America.

One hopes to see sustained reform in the political, social, and educational fields too. This will make a difference. Japan enjoys long traditions of course, but her society is becoming more transparent. Lifetime employment is changing. Restructuring is starting to bite. Women are advancing. Social problems are now more freely debated. There is structured comparison of notes with European partners. Common themes - health, population, social insurance - emerge increasingly. Domestic politics are rightly regarded as an area for change by the world's press. During my time, Japan saw five prime ministers. None completely cracked the domestic political restructuring problem. But there were significant changes in electoral law and campaign funding. New external policy requirements developed, bringing their own lessons for domestic management.

I would still be delighted to see Japan as a Permanent Member of the Security Council. She should continue to help the international community to pick up a security burden that can seem exhausting to us all. It is vitally important of course to keep the US well placed as a stabilizing factor in Asia.

But the long-term is not a given. Asia as a whole is evolving. It is not naïve optimism, I hope, to say that on the whole the open society is gaining. Indonesia has voted for a new president. A real political process is at work in Taiwan. The British press has spotted an element of reality in village democracy in China. These changes are good, not because they are Western but because they give people a better deal. And people are now remarkably well-informed about alternatives. IT carries its own message. Communications monopolies are collapsing, driven by technical options and simple economics. China itself is rapidly increasing cable systems. Allegedly one hundred million people are on-line. Networking between Chinese universities is a major fact. In the world as a whole, the opening of society can be problematic but lack of communication is worse.

Global process drives so much. But, between Asia and Europe, economics are not enough. The relationship is still weak institutionally. We need to develop deeper Asia-Europe links across the range for a more stable world. We have to give the relationship a substance and a flavour that convinces constituencies at both ends. We can neither leave all the management burdens to one superpower or fail to protect Europe's stake in the resolution of issues yet to come.

BUILDING THE RELATIONSHIP

How should we aim to build up this relationship? By effort. Take Japan as an example. While I was there I saw visits by a large proportion of the British Cabinet of the day, far from limited to foreign affairs and trade. Forty ministers in all came to Tokyo, with emphasis on functional exchanges as well as social and educational links. Exchanges flourished on global security too. (Britain thinks blue water as well as land mass). Our shared addiction to innovative science was reflected in excellent research links and an Agreement.

I see an encouraging echo in Cambridge: Labs have been funded, there is a strong Japanese presence on the Science Park, individual collaborations flourish on new materials and engine technology. Presidents of Asian universities visit my College. We have Japanese and Chinese members on the Fellowship. Students from Asia, undergraduate and graduate, make a strong intellectual contribution. It is a general good to bring next generation talent forward.

In sum, Europe as a whole needs a solid long-term relationship with Asia. Both of us face a huge menu of practical problems, centring on the state of a shared world and the question of whether our species will survive. Asia and Europe have a contribution to make in partnership, playing to their respective strengths. We should both use our imagination. We should look ahead. We should actively develop a common agenda. We should run with themes, which speak to the next generation.

In this context the Vision Group exercise was hugely welcome. ASEM is of course a process rather than a structure, our Report being one contribution. We have seen a rising graph of results from the meeting in Bangkok (1996), through London (1998), leading to Seoul 2000. The 'road map' commissioned at the second meeting, was submitted in Berlin. Other events competed, but I hope that it did not pass unnoticed. It will I believe have nourished the Asia-Europe thought process.

In a sense the Report heightens the obvious. But the exercise itself pulled us into shared focus, looking at the Asia-Europe relationship as a whole and highlighting the potential for development. The key, for Europeans, is working with Asia not just on Asia. The Report reflected a shared wish for a much closer link, different in quality and quantity, looking forward, drawing heavily on technology. There is clearly a joint will to strengthen the third side of the global triangle and a refusal to be deflected. For me the key features of the Vision Group Report are:

(1) Support for open solutions - a collective view that we need to reinforce the multilateral trading system and promote the success of the next international trade round. We set an eventual goal of free trade in goods and services by 2025. We proposed a strategic framework. We similarly took an open view of the global financial system, hoping to see a particular effort by Asia and Europe to work together. Both of us need more transparent and efficient money management.

The Report reflects strong enthusiasm for mutual investment between Asia and Europe and proposes a variety of devices to promote trade and investment both ways. We proposed a trade week. We proposed business councils. The Report devotes much attention to infrastructural improvements, notably in transport and energy. We share a strong wish to see improved technology for communications. The main burden is the need for concrete steps.

(2) A second key feature is the focus on social betterment, including governance and human rights. This is always a ticklish area. Nevertheless the Report reflects joint treatment. We deliberately chose the sub-title *For a better tomorrow*. We want to see principles of good governance affirmed at next Summit. We want to see NGOs as well as Governments involved in political and security dialogue. We recommend more work on values and the promotion of a dialogue that will genuinely underpin security. There is a firm call for solidarity on human rights, refugee movements, and women's' rights, and a particular concern for issues of social imbalance. In my reading, we are looking for practical ways to give people the rights they deserve. This is not a new idea but it takes up the theme of 'societies in transition'.

(3) Education is a central concern. It is not hard to guess my own views. We should use all the modern means available to expand educational opportunity in both Europe and Asia and meaningful interchange between the two. The Vision Group wants to see this theme profiled at Seoul. Europe and Asia will both be skilled societies - or of no use. We must develop an ability to compare notes, and an institutional framework. The Group hope to see a fivefold increase in students exchanged between Europe and Asia by 2025. We seek a much better balance each way. It is vital of course for Europe to attract its share of Asian talent. We are particularly attached to the recommendation for a high profile scholarship scheme between Europe and Asia, initially at graduate level. Look what Senator Fulbright did for long-term relations with the US. We hope to see this project endorsed by ASEM leaders.

In parallel we favour a drive for closer contacts between ASEM education ministers and university heads. We want to see student mobility increased. This means more transparency, new degree systems and less bureaucracy. There is food for discussion here among Europeans themselves as well as between Europe and Asia. We also believe that exchanges should begin early on in the school career. IT must be used to the full. Efforts should be made to establish visiting professorships and promote a variety of societal exchanges.

(4) Let me reiterate the significance of IT. Its dynamic potential has emerged even further since the Vision Group Report. There is huge global competition in software, where Europe can also shine. The specialist press tells us that possibilities for e-business as well as e-commerce are in their infancy but will advance rapidly and transform global prospects. Distance is already vanishing. Outward processing is an example. I myself am particularly interested in the language implications. The Nuffield Languages

Inquiry in the UK has thrown up many points, among them the very strong global role of English. I cannot believe though that Europe will not want to keep up strong expertise in Asian languages and culture. This is essential to comprehensive understanding and is reflected in evolving patterns of support for higher education in my own country.

(5) The strong perception of the environmental imperative. If this does not drive Europe and Asia to co-operate, nothing else will. Failure to tackle the present agenda could bring us all down. Appalling urban degradation and failure to resolve basics of energy, water, and waste marks the late twentieth century world. Too many concrete examples, both Asian and European, are at hand. The 'problem of the city' should be a common theme. It is urgent to implement existing international agreements and find effective ways to preserve our natural resources.

(6) The Report contains many recommendations, across a broad range, some institutional and others substantive. We aim to make a difference. But this is not just a matter for drafting groups; a major move on Europe-Asia relations will rest on people. Let us not forget the role of ASEF. There is much that it can do - promotion of cultural contact, concrete arrangements for twinning, the effort to seek joint advantage in terms and in activities that people understand. In areas in which Europe itself has pulled itself together, or the reverse, lessons can be drawn.

MATCHING CONFUCIUS WITH VIRGIL

Finally, let me stress, first, that it cannot be assumed that all European ideas are good for Asia. Modesty should prevail. Why should our Asian partners want to work with us? They can see after all the strong competition from a vibrant North American society. The US economy has done far better than European or Asian critics were suggesting when I went to Japan, and that is already half a dozen years ago. Nevertheless there are reasons for us in Europe to focus closely on our links with Asia:

(a) A broadening of Asia's options also broadens ours;
(b) Asian partners will work with us if we go for open systems. The idea of a protectionist Asia is largely behind us. But it should be acceptable at neither end;
(c) Our partners will work with us if we stay smart. We need to look to our own backyard. To repeat, the Vision Group Report is very open in spirit.

They will not want to work with us if we are boring. Bright Asian colleagues will come to European campuses if we continue to generate good ideas. We are after all the societies of Leonardo, Descartes, Newton, and Leibnitz. I see daily reminders, where I live, of Darwin, Herschel, and Crick. But there can be no resting on our laurels. You will all remember Rip van Winkle, who woke up to find the world utterly unrecognizable. If our ideas dry up so will their interest and their visits. The global system allows talent to crop up and express itself virtually anywhere. We have to remain excellent.

My last thought is this. We the Europeans have to concentrate and work together on extracting maximum advantage from our relationship with Asia. We need to ensure that the relationship is actively embraced in our institutions, shared or national. And we have to retain not just pride in our own cultures but a determination to keep them up to the mark. We need to generate the skills to guarantee this.

There is much to work on here. The Vision Group Report points out that both Europe and Asia can draw from deep wells. We can match their Confucius with our Virgil. There was a measure of mutual support between the Roman Empire and the very humanistic Han. Now, 2000 years later, I expect Europe-Asia to be a continuing theme. If the Group's recommendations flourish, I expect to see many more conferences like this.

CHAPTER 3

FOR A BETTER TOMORROW: ASIA-EUROPE PARTNERSHIP IN THE 21ST CENTURY

ROBERT S. ARENDAL

President Kim Young Sam of the Republic of Korea first proposed the Asian European Vision Group, also referred to as 'The Vision Group' or abbreviated as AEVG, in 1996. It was acceded the support of the Foreign Ministers of ASEM in 1997. The Vision Group was officially formed at the second Asia-Europe Summit Meeting, held in London in April 1998 at the special request of the Heads of State of ASEM. The Vision Group is composed of twenty-six members, each representing one of the ASEM countries.

The AEVG held its first meeting in 1998 and this has been followed by four other meetings under the chairmanship of Dr Il SaKong, former Minister of Finance of Korea. The Vision Group's report under the heading 'For a Better Tomorrow - Asia-Europe Partnership in the 21st Century' will be presented at the ASEM Summit Meeting in October 2000 in Korea. It is expected that the Heads of State will give their comments.

OVERARCHING VIEW

The Vision Group strongly endorses the view that the ASEM process has made an admirable start, with initiatives involving not only governments but in which the business sector plays a valiant role especially in the fields of culture, the arts and society issues. The Vision Group also believes that ASEM activities must be seen in a longer perspective; there is much to be done to intensify and deepen relations between Asia and Europe - and the goodwill is there.

Of paramount importance to economic growth and prosperity is a closer relation between us which must rest on better awareness and understanding of the cultures of our two regions. Hence the emphasis placed on people-to-people relations as well as education and science. The Report is inspired by the conviction that the ASEM process now requires an overarching vision of Asia-Europe relations in the long-term. Consequently, if the ASEM leaders accept the report, this vision can help to shape the directions of Asia-Europe relations over the next century.

At present Asia and Europe find themselves in the midst of an economic, social and communications revolution, a revolution which is set to accelerate. This poses new challenges in the twenty-first century. Given their history, cultural strengths and talents, it is imperative that Asia and Europe work together to make a strong and specific contribution, by addressing these issues with urgency and tenacity.

Since the inaugural meeting of ASEM leaders in Bangkok in 1996, the ASEM process has got off to a good start. However, it is far from enough. After four years, it is time to move on to a new and deeper phase of Asia-Europe relations. This second phase needs to be guided by an overarching vision which articulates the overall goal of strengthening relations between the two regions. It should be the vision which drives the process, and not vice versa.

AEVG's vision is gradually to integrate Asia and Europe into an area of peace and shared development, a prosperous common living sphere in the twenty-first century. This is a sphere in which our knowledge, wealth, cultural heritage, democratic ideals, educational assets, intellectual aspirations, and our new technologies are closely intertwined and exchanged, unhampered by specific barriers or constraints. We envision the active integration of our intellectual forces and a vibrant exchange of culture and the arts between Asia and Europe. We hold before us a correction of today's imbalance in student numbers between Europe and Asia, with a five-fold expansion in student exchanges between the two regions by the year 2025. We also visualize the progressive opening of markets with the eventual goal of free flow of goods and services by the year 2025. Integral to our vision are concrete actions to meet the serious environmental challenges to the world today.

MAJOR RECOMMENDATIONS:

- Eventual Goal of Free Trade in Goods & Services by 2025
- Closer Macroeconomic Policy Co-ordination and Reform of the Inter national Financial System
- Asia-Europe Business Advisory Council
- Improved ASEM Infrastructure Framework
- ASEM Information Technology Council
- ASEM Environment Centre
- Declaration on Education
- ASEM Scholarship Programme
- Affirmation of the Principles of Good Governance

Other Recommendations:

- Progress at the next Round of International Trade Talks
- Global Rules for Enhancing Transparency and Prudent Financial Supervision
- Asia-Europe Trade Week
- ASEM Work Programme on Electronic Commerce
- Promoting Investment
- ASEM Advisory Network of Senior Executives
- Aviation Agreements and Aerospace Development
- Energy Co-operation
- Virtual Technology Transfer Centre and Co-operation between Technology Transfer Centres
- 'Non-Marketable' Technologies-Solutions in Health Care
- Co-operation in Economic Assistance
- Forum of ASEM Education Ministers and Heads of Universities
- Dual Degree, Targeted Language Teaching, Simplification of National Academic Regulations, and Survey of Curricula
- Establishment of ASEM Visiting Professorships
- Forum for Societal Exchanges - Strengthening ASEF
- Biennial ASEM Cultural Festival
- ASEM Twin Cities
- Political and Security Dialogue
- Designation of Joint Training Centres and Facilities for Peacekeeping Operations
- Strengthened Dialogue among Asian Countries
- Managing Social Imbalances
- ASEM Secretariat

The Environmental Challenge and the Enhancement of Educational, cultural and Social Exchanges

One of the key priorities on the global action agenda is the enormous environmental challenge which both industrialized and developing countries face today. The Vision Group proposes that ASEM develop closer long-term environmental co-operation: defining priority areas and objectives, with annual reviews, along with specific measures to attain these objectives; developing institutional capacity competent to implement environmental policies. In order to realize these goals by means of concrete co-operation, and to ensure symmetry with other current environmental programmes outside the ambit of ASEM, the Vision Group recommends the establishment of an ASEM Environment Centre.

The Vision Group believes that educational exchanges lie at the heart of achieving a deeper understanding between Asia and Europe. To this end, we urge ASEM Leaders, at their meeting in Seoul in 2000, to issue an ASEM Declaration on Education. Our vision regarding educational exchanges is three-fold: a significantly better balance in student numbers between Europe and Asia within the next five years; a five-fold increase in the total number of students exchanged between Europe and Asia by the year 2025; and an improved balance between the numbers of Asian foreign students studying in North America and those studying in Europe.

A clear signal of the commitment of ASEM governments to the development of young talent and leadership potential on both sides is now urgent. The Vision Group recommends the creation of a prestigious, high-profile ASEM Scholarship Scheme. ASEM scholarships will be awarded to the best and brightest of students chosen for their quality of intellect and level of attainment for postgraduate study on an inter-regional basis.

The Vision Group proposes that the Asia-Europe Foundation (ASEF) be strengthened, so that it is better able to carry out an extended objective of promoting cultural co-operation and exchange between Asia and Europe. This can be done at ASEM 3 after ASEF submits a report card on its visions, achievements, and aspirations. We also propose a biennial ASEM cultural festival and the establishment of ASEM twin cities.

PROMOTING POLITICAL AND SECURITY CO-OPERATION

In order to promote better understanding between the two regions subscribing to the guiding principles laid down in the Bangkok Summit, the Vision Group sees the dialogue between Asia and Europe on good governance in international relations as part of their political co-operation. The Vision Group therefore recommends that at their meeting in Seoul in 2000 ASEM Leaders affirm the principles of good governance.

Given the importance of political and security issues, ASEM should lend itself as a vehicle for political and security dialogue between Asia and Europe at different levels, and encourage, co-ordinate and support the involvement of both governmental and non-governmental organizations in political and security dialogue. ASEM partners could also explore ways and means to promote co-operation between the ASEAN Regional Forum (ARF) and the Organisation for Security and Co-operation in Europe (OSCE).

Firstly, we need to start with: Liberalization and Open Markets; we need to ensure that liberalization will continue and that protectionism will diminish. It is critical for ASEM partners to undertake early action to reinforce the multilateral trading system and to co-operate to achieve, as soon as possible, the success of the next rounds of international trade talks.

Secondly, we need to assure an Asia-Europe Co-operation for Financial Stability; the Vision Group welcomes the introduction of the Euro, and calls for closer macroeconomic policy co-ordination between the major economic players. In the area of international finance, we see a need for Asia and Europe to work even more closely together in order to achieve a co-ordinated response in step with rapid financial globalization.

Globalization of the world economy is destined to intensify in the twenty-first century. In an inexorably globalizing world, national economies will face difficulty fostering economic development simply by relying exclusively on domestic resources. Both Asia and Europe have benefited tremendously from the economic liberalization of the past few decades. The Vision Group calls upon ASEM partners to resist protectionist measures. We shall all best be served by focusing on continued liberalization in trade and investment. It is critical for ASEM partners to undertake early action to reinforce the multilateral trading system and to co-operate to achieve the success of the next round of international trade talks as soon as possible.

The Vision Group recommends that ASEM partners set the eventual goal of free trade in goods and services by the year 2025 by adopting a strategic framework for the progressive freeing of trade in goods and services among themselves. The successful building of this framework is necessary in order for the European-Asian Business Community to play a creative and dynamic role in developing beneficial contribution to all the partners. The Group noted that Asia-Europe trade had increased significantly, enhancing Asia-Europe Trade and Investments.

While appreciating the many initiatives which the ASEM partners have launched (such as the Investment Promotion Action Plan (IPAP), the Trade Facilitation Action Plan (TFAP), and other such as the Asia-Europe Environmental Technology Centre (AEETC) and ASEMConnect), the Group believes that these must be urgently implemented and expanded even more to have a significant effect on trade and investment.

The Vision Group urges ASEM partners to launch an Asia-Europe Trade Week (AETW). Held bi-annually, in alternating locations between Asia and Europe, starting from the year 2002 and in conjunction with the ASEM Summit, the AETW should aim to contribute to a business environment that will foster increased trade between the two regions.

The AETW should comprise business symposia, industry tours, business councils, Technomart (a technology exhibition), and trade fairs. By providing information and services to expand business opportunities, the AETW can also support business co-operation to enhance economic growth across ASEM. In order to distinguish itself from conference-type activities, the AETW would be organized around trade fairs, supplemented by a variety of business-oriented events. Each AETW could then focus on a specific industry pre-identified as having the potential to boost Asia-Europe trade flows. Each AETW can be organized by the host country of ASEM in co-ordination with the Asia-Europe Business Forum.

The Asia-Europe Vision Group also recommends that ASEM launch a work programme on electronic commerce, calling for contributions from international bodies. It urges members to educate current and potential users of electronic commerce in order to realise its economic and social benefits more speedily in both Europe and Asia. A global framework for rule setting and enforcement leading to an international convention in this area should be actively sought by ASEM partners, working together.

Electronic commerce provides a fundamentally new way of conducting commercial transactions and forging new and more direct relationships between businesses, consumers, and governments. In order to realize the potential of electronic commerce, governments must recognize the leading role of the business sector. Where legislation is necessary, rules should be simple, balanced, and within a legal framework that retains its consistence across international borders. In the absence of such a framework, e-commerce will take longer to become fully accepted.

There is a need to open up local markets to foreign investors. The Vision Group stresses the importance of ensuring an attractive investment climate in order to increase Foreign Direct Investment (FDI) flows between ASEM partners. In all these areas, the Vision Group recommends ASEM partners benchmark their investment policies and regulations against those of countries, which are considered to be particularly successful among ASEM partners.

The Vision Group recommends that the ASEM Leaders establish Asia-Europe Business Advisory Councils (BACs). With the intention of extending BACs to all Asian and European partners, the Group initially suggests that one be set up in each region. The main objective of the BACs would be to institute high level dialogue to promote Asia-Europe investment, with a membership including national government leaders and the CEOs of companies, domestic and foreign. The Asia-Europe BAC in each country can also act as a forum for foreign investors in that country in which common problems relating to the investment climate can be discussed, and by which advice on critical investment, trade and market access related issues can be given to governments and regulators. The scope of the Asia-Europe BACs would range over different key areas, such as intellectual property rights, market access, deregulation, infrastructure, land rights, and company ownership.

To promote business opportunities and cross-border investment in ASEM partners by SMEs, which face special difficulties, the Group seeks formation of an ASEM Advisory Network of Senior Executives (ANSE), a non-profit association of active and/or retired executives on a non-profit basis who can share their wealth of experience and business know-how in an interactive forum with small businesses. The aim is to help SMEs decide on how, where, when, and with whom to engage in business and investment, and how best to explore strategic alliances and market opportunities.

AN IMPROVED ASEM INFRASTRUCTURE

The Vision Group recommends that ASEM adopt an improved ASEM infrastructure framework for all key areas (energy, telecommunications, transport, water, environment, and so forth), which are critical to inter-regional trade, technology sharing, and investor confidence. This implies the following main actions:

- Substantial public policy reforms such as sustained infrastructure liberalization and stabilization, including freeing prices, trade and the entry of new market players;
- benchmarking the current status of, especially the large gaps existing in, ASEM public-private infrastructure financing needs, legal forms of partnerships, guarantee instruments (e.g. EIB, ADB, WB, IFC) and anti-corruption measures taken by the World Bank (WB), the Asian Development Bank (ADB), and the OECD; and
- systematic cost-benefit analysis of the most viable infrastructure projects since the volume of both public and private co-financing for ASEM projects is often lower than the number of projects identified.

The Vision Group especially cites initiatives in transport and energy, both areas with very large demands on capital. The vision group recommends that all modes of transport between Asia and Europe be expanded through greater liberalization. Protectionism must be eliminated and free competition among carriers be encouraged by introducing measures such as transparency in tendering and procurement procedures.

As an example, we highlight air cargo - one of the fastest growing modes of transport. Globalization, just-in-time manufacturing and distribution, as well as increased competition are factors leading exporters and importers in

Asia and Europe to become increasingly dependent on air cargo. E-commerce will boost this sector even more.

Consequently The Vision Group makes a specific recommendation that the ASEM partners negotiate liberalized aviation agreements. Liberalisation should be accompanied parallel by joint meetings of the ASEM partners to review airport planning and investment requirements within and between the ASEM partners, also with the aim of maximizing the positive impact of infrastructural investment throughout the two regions. The Vision Group also argues strongly for the strengthening of co-operation in aerospace development especially in aerospace component production and heavy maintenance centres serving all types of aircraft.

Energy is another important area in which the Group believes ASEM partners should co-operate to their mutual benefit. There are at least four possible areas of ASEM co-operation for energy-related technology and infrastructure development:

- It is essential to expand the use of natural gas. This requires strengthening the supply infrastructure, both cross-border pipelines and LNG infrastructure. International co-operation is bound to become increasingly important, especially private sector participation in both LNG and pipeline infrastructure.
- Nuclear power remains important as an energy source. Use of nuclear power, however, demands the highest standards of nuclear safety and full safeguards under the terms of agreements with the International Atomic Energy Agency (IAEA). To build trust and confidence, both domestically and with neighbours, transparency in nuclear materials handling is also a vital criterion, as is effective waste management.
- The use of coal offers many advantages, as its cost is low and supply is stable. From an environmental point of view, however, numerous problems remain before pollution can be minimized. It is crucial to develop Asian-European co-operation on both new clean coal technology and high efficiency coal combustion technologies.
- Renewable energy sources such as wind, solar, and biomass should be jointly developed and implemented wherever possible.

The Vision Group proposes that an ASEM Information Technology Council be formed comprising members from both the public and private sectors to promote information infrastructure development in such areas as technical standards, electronic translation software, and satellite TV broadcasting.

INCREASING CO-OPERATION AND PARTNERSHIP

Last but not least, I would like to mention two important prerequisites for the expansion of the co-operation and partnership of Asia and Europe. The first is the ASEM process. The Vision Group is strongly of the opinion that the ASEM process is valuable and must continue, forging into the future. It notes three features affecting the long-term development of ASEM.

There needs to be a greater awareness of ASEM among populations of the ASEM partners. The ASEM process has to move beyond government circles. There needs to be a greater engagement of the business sector, of society and, above all, of the people of our two regions. Secondly, in addition to meetings of ASEM Ministers of Foreign Affairs, Economic and Finance, the Vision Group recommends meetings of ministers responsible for the Environment, Science, Technology, and Education to cement deepening political and social interaction between the two regions. Thirdly, there could be an expansion of the membership of ASEM.

Given these three considerations, the Vision Group believes that the ASEM process will become more complex, not less. The Vision Group cautions that the current institutional framework is insufficient and likely to constrain the positive evolution of the ASEM process. There is now a need for a point of co-ordination, a focus for continuity ensuring the momentum of the ASEM process and for maintaining communication on ASEM activities and achievements. Such a point of co-ordination should have the ability to set a timetable and ensure that it is maintained. The Vision Group therefore recommends the establishment of a lean but effective secretariat.

The second point is the strengthening and expansion of The Asia-European Business Forum (AEBF). The Vision Group did not give any specific recommendations on the AEBF, as it is already established and functioning. However, my personal opinion is that the AEBF is an excellent opportunity to further expand the trade relations between Asia and Europe to new heights. It is an ideal event to review the progress made in the various specific trade relations and business co-operations as it is a joint effort of both the business community and the ASEM governments. The AEBF can play a very significant role in developing - expanded and improved trade as well as business relations between the two regions, - and it can also become a vehicle on which to build an even stronger and equally successful trade relations like the ties that have already been created between the US and Asia. But to do so, it needs two key ingredients: a stronger involvement in and commitment from the business community. Without the active and may I call it enthusiastic support of the private sector, the AEBF will not play the dynamic role it so easily could. Such support from the private sector would be vital to improving the business and trade relationship between Asia and Europe. Consequently, the AEBF needs - like the ASEM process itself - an AEBF Secretariat or co-ordination office.

While I appreciate and fully support the initiatives that the governments of ASEM provide - especially the host-governments - it seems that there is a lack of AEBF activities between each event and insufficient communication and co-ordination. I believe this matter could easily be solved by such a co-ordination office and most likely, with a direct link to improved and expanded trade between Asia and Europe. An AEBF co-ordination office could be established in co-operation with the ASEM governments and the ASEM private sector, or there might be possibilities to have the co-ordination out-sourced, let's say, to the Chamber of Commerce of the ASEM countries or similar sorts of organizations. Whatever the solution, we must take action in both the ASEM process itself as well as in the AEBF process. And in both cases the private sector of the Europe-Asia Business Community as well as the ASEM government involvement is equally important. Last but not least, what is the role that each country can play in the ASEM process and in developing the relationship between Asia and Europe?

1. Each member country must be more visible in the Asia-Europe co-operation. At the Summit meeting in London in 1998, Singapore presented a website for ASEM countries. Each ASEM member should be represented on this website - it is good publicity, and it can promote business as well as social and cultural relationship with Asia.
2. Each ASEM partner should take a more active part in the ASEM process, support the recommendations made by the AEVG as well as the many other recommendations made by ASEM itself, the EU, and by the European and Asian countries
3. European ASEM members should undertake even more trade promotion activities in Asia and vice versa. The Board of Economic Developments could do this, as it has been doing very successfully in the past, as well as by the Chamber of Commerce and with the support of the ASEM members' embassies in Asia.
4. Likewise, encouraging Asian promoters to stay in Luxembourg could be equally successful.
5. Last but not least, Trade Week Events and Advisory Councils as recom-mended by the Vision Group could be other ways to expand the relation-ship between Europe and Asia, in the spirit of the ASEM process.

It is better to act now than later. By strengthening the co-operation and the ties between Asia and Europe today we shall all achieve a better tomorrow.

PART TWO
REALIZING ASEM'S POTENTIAL

CHAPTER 4

RESOLVING THE PARADOX

ANTHONY MURPHY

The striking paradox underlying the relationship between the Government and the private sectors in ASEM is that they consider the interaction between Government and the business community in ASEM to be one of the forum's greatest strengths but yet it is seen by some as one of the forum's most serious weaknesses - so serious indeed that it threatens to undermine the ASEM process altogether or at least reduce it to little more than another talking-shop for politicians and officials.

Personally, I do not subscribe to the more extreme versions of this pessimistic view. We should be careful not to belittle the significant achievements of the three Business Forums which have already taken place - in Paris, Bangkok and London; or prejudice the success of the Forums still to come - in Korea, Austria, and Singapore. But resolving the paradox seems to me to be one of the most important challenges facing ASEM today - at stake is the credibility of ASEM as an outward-looking, broad-based forum in which business people take an active and influential role.

TASKS AHEAD

That this is a task worth doing is not, I believe, in doubt. But it might be worth reminding ourselves why developing the dialogue between Government and the business community is important.

First, the business community can help to ensure that work carried out on the Government side of ASEM remains firmly anchored in reality, in the needs and concerns of the men and women primarily responsible for developing a flourishing trade and investment relationship between Asia and Europe - what in APEC is called the Reality Check.

Second, there is no doubt that work done by officials in such ereas as trade and investment facilitation derives focus and value from the practical experience of business people. There is nothing in the background of even the most experienced and conscientious official to match the insights of people whose daily lives are spent dealing with barriers to trade and investment.

Third, dialogue with business allows Government to devote scarce resources to wherever these are most needed. In the sphere of trade facilitation alone, the range and diversity of the barriers facing business is huge: customs procedures, intellectual property protection, standards and technical regulations, government procurement - all areas encompassed in the ASEM Trade Facilitation Action Plan (TFAP). Business can help direct regulators and enforcers towards the area where progress needs to be made.

Fourth, the business community can use its significant leverage to help overcome the reluctance and outright resistance of officials who are otherwise unconvinced of the need for change. ASEM is a diverse body of countries and not every country shares the liberal, pro-business agenda of the UK And this leverage extends not just to the details of trade and investment facilitation but also to the big overarching issues - not least the collective ASEM approach to the onset of a new round of multilateral trade negotiations in the WTO next year.

And fifth, bringing business into the Asia-Europe dialogue broadens the basis which over time ASEM will need to develop and contribute towards what I have called ASEM Democracy - an inclusive outward-looking forum based on respect for diversity but united by a wide range of shared interests.

Against such a background it is puzzling that some commentators have observed an apparent waning in business support for ASEM. The Federation of Korean Industries will be hosting the fourth Business Forum in Seoul in 2000 and has put in place an impressive organisation to ensure the meeting is a success. But the response so far has been lethargic to say the least. Several of the six Working Groups around which the main business of the Forum will revolve are undersubscribed. Some countries have so far only provided the names of one or two delegates, others - six EU countries and three Asian - none at all. I am sure that over the next few months the momentum will increase. But it remains surprising that, three years into a process that began in Paris in 1996 with such high hopes and expectations, the reaction of business is so muted.

WANING BUSINESS SUPPORT FOR ASEM?

Why should this be? Are we seeing here another manifestation of the fall-out from the Asian financial crisis and its repercussions across the globe? I do not think so - even though many businesses have suffered severely, others have been quick to capitalize on the opportunities created by depreciated assets and currencies to trade and invest. Among the reasons cited are:

Business Fatigue. It may well be true that in seeking to extend and diversify their dialogue with the business community, governments in Europe and Asia have misjudged the readiness of firms to devote time to conferences, seminars, outward investment missions and so on. Since the second ASEM Summit fourteen months ago the UK has dispatched two major high-level business missions to Korea, and now we are recruiting volunteers for the Forum in the autumn. Has business had enough?

Lack of resources. Not all companies are as well-resourced with managers as bureaucracies are - sometimes - with civil servants. Even in the largest companies, the pressures of the past decade to cut costs and become more competitive have reduced the ability of companies to support anything that lies outside their core profit-making activities.

Lack of Focus. The Asia-Europe Business Forum (AEBF) is seen rightly as the main channel of dialogue between Government and business in ASEM. But the strong and natural desire of countries to be seen to be contributing something led to the holding of events which, if not actually rivals to the mainstream Forum process, have certainly brought about a division of forces - for example the Business Conference in Jakarta in 1997 and the Asia-Europe SUE Conference in Naples last year. The Decision-Makers Round Table which will take place in Seoul immediately after the fourth Business Forum will undoubtedly draw heavily on attendance at the Forum but is actually a distinct activity conceived under the Investment Promotion Action Plan (IPAP) The Vision Group has proposed new business-related entities and events: Business Advisory Councils, a twice-yearly Asia-Europe Trade Week, and an Advisory Network of senior Executives. All worthy and important ideas - but likely to blur the focus still further.

Lack of engagement at the national level? I put a question mark here because I did not want to be dogmatic about the situation in other countries. I know that our own CBI regularly attends meetings of UNICE, the European employers' federation. But I am not sure to what extent across the breadth of ASEM national federations and the individual companies they represent are literate in ASEM issues.

Lack of continuity. A frequent criticism of the Business Forum is that ideas and initiatives developed in one Forum are not carried over to the next. We see this in the themes proposed for the Working Groups, which form the core of all Forum activity. Some have achieved a kind of mo-mentum - for example financial services others - tourism, and the sectoral Groups formed at the London Forum - have blossomed only briefly. It is natural that the organizers of each Forum should want their event to have its own unique character - indeed even to be an arena for some national hobbyhorses. But if good ideas are withering on the vine then something is going wrong.

Lack of feedback is closely related to lack of continuity. Even the best ideas will fail if no one bothers to pick them up and carry them forward. And even the worst merit some acknowledgement from Government.

So what can we do to address these problems? One approach is to look at how the Government-to-business dialogue is handled in other similar forums, such as the APEC Business Advisory Council (ABAC) and the Transatlantic Business Dialogues (TABD).

COMPARABLE GOVERNMENT-BUSINESS ORGANIZATIONS

Looking at ABAC (founded in 1995) first, APEC contains twenty-one member economies and each provides three senior business representatives to the Council (contrast this with twenty-six partners in ASEM each having to supply six or seven people for the next Forum). The chairmanship mirrors the overall chairmanship of APEC - Philip Burdon of New Zealand is the current chair and will hand over to a Bruneian successor at the end of the year. This creates, I believe, the opportunity for closer business-to-Government co-ordination.

ABAC has produced three major reports on the theme of 'APEC Means Business' since 1996 covering such big issues as the Asian financial crisis and economic and technical co-operation in APEC - ECOTECH. The Council meets more regularly than its ASEM counterpart - three times this year, in Bandar Seri Begawan in February, in Tokyo in May and in Auckland in September, just before the meeting of APEC Economic Leaders. And ABAC has been strongly proactive in monitoring the progress of work on the Government side of ASEM, commenting through the Action Plan Monitoring Committee on the progress of individual actions of member economies plus (IAPAs), and - most significantly - on APEC's record in implementing ABAC recommendations, APEC also runs an on-line Business Centre which includes an investment guidebook, labour market information, and data on government procurement practices and opportunities. And ABAC boasts a permanent International Secretariat - based in Makati City in the Philippines - which works closely with the main APEC Secretariat in Singapore.

So ABAC has a number of interesting features. What about the TABD (established in 1995). It is presided over by two co-chairs, one from the EU and one from the US. Meetings are held annually, and the focus is very much on business-to-business interaction - though when the TABD last met, last November in Charlotte, North Carolina, the Ministerial and senior official presence was almost overwhelming: Gore, Daley, Barshefsky, Eizenstat, Summers for the US, Brittan and Bangemann for the EU.

The TABD covers a mix of cross-cutting issues like metrification as well as industry specific issues. One of its principal achievements was to bring its considerable leverage to bear on the conclusion of the EU/US Mutual Recognition Agreement in May 1998. The TABD runs small secretariats on each side of the Atlantic, funded by the two companies providing the co-chairs but - interestingly - made up of the same people irrespective of the source of funding.

Now, I am not saying that either ABAC or the TABD is a more effective organisation than the Asia-Europe Business Forum. But there are enough differences in the way the three forums organize themselves to prompt the question: 'What can we learn or borrow from other forums to make the AEBF a more focused and influential force in the sphere of Asia-Europe relations?'

LESSONS FROM ABAC AND TABD

First, there is clearly a case to be made for defining a limited number of core principles which will ensure that successive Forums are united by elements of common identity - without in any way eroding the right of the organizers to give each Forum a distinct personality. I believe it is for business itself to define what those principles might be, and I am glad that the Federation of Korean industries is taking the initiative to define a framework of guidelines to foster continuity between one Forum and another.

Second, there is a strong case to be made for closer correlation between the respective work programmes of the Business Forum and the Government side of ASEM, notably in the area of the trade facilitation and investment promotion action plans which form the twin key elements of the economic work programme in ASEM. Business has a vital role to play in steering and stimulating work in this area, identifying priorities, and in helping to overcome the reluctance of less liberal partners - though the Forum should also be creative in developing new areas and encouraging Government to follow - a case of the flag following trade, rather than trade following the flag.

As I have already mentioned, I should like to see national federations involving themselves and their members more closely in the Forum process, acting as conduits for two-way information flows.

Providing feedback is, I believe, a vital pan of the framework. Business people are naturally pragmatists: if an idea simply will not work in practice, or has been tried already and failed, they will accept this and move on. But failing to react to business ideas is tantamount to disparaging the work invested in them: at best, government can be accused of a lack of courtesy, at worst persistently ignoring business views creates antagonism, indifference, and an eventual breakdown in dialogue. So the idea that the four co-ordinators on the Government side of ASEM - the Commission, the incumbent EU Presidency, Thailand and Korea - should function as a clearinghouse, collating and evaluating business-generated ideas, and ultimately providing feedback is a good one.

I also feel that the credibility of the ASEM process would be greatly reinforced if a systematic effort were made to quantify the benefits flowing from, or expected to flow from, initiatives taken in the economic area. This would provide ASEM with a yardstick for measuring its own effectiveness in meeting the targets set by leaders, and an incentive to the business community to maintain their involvement in a forum which was self-evidently supporting them and their businesses.

Finally, I believe a major effort needs to be made to ensure that SMEs are fully integrated into the ASEM process - to think small. No one can deny that small companies face particular difficulties in coping with the array of market access barriers, which still impede trade and investment in many parts of the world. The needs of SMEs have featured prominently in the rhetoric of ASEM. But much more has to be done by Government and business to bring SMEs into the centre of the debate. Behind the business delegates who attended the forums in Paris and Bangkok and London lies a vast hinterland of corporate activity largely untouched by the ASEM process - a reservoir of experience and insight, which ASEM needs to tap into for the sake of its own credibility. A Working Group dedicated to the concerns of SMEs will form part of the fourth Business Forum in Seoul. I hope this Group will focus not just on the problems small businesses face, but also on the task of bringing SMEs into the light.

I hope I have been able to share with you some ideas and insights about the role of business in the Asia-Europe relationship and how the Business Forum process might be made more effective. What I have offered is a personal view based on observation of two Forums and close involvement in preparations for a third. Some nettles - such as the case for creating a permanent secretariat on the ABAC model - I have left deliberately ungrasped. But let me close by saying that I firmly believe that the business community has a massive contribution to make to the vitality of the ASEM process, by generating ideas, coaxing and sometimes coercing Government into action, and above all ensuring that ASEM remains outward-looking and tethered to the granite of hard economic reality.

CHAPTER 5

THE ASEM PROCESS:
NEW RULES FOR ENGAGEMENT IN A GLOBAL
ENVIRONMENT*

LEO SCHMIT

In 1994 the Council of the European Union adopted the New Asia Strategy document stating the Union's commitment to improving its relations with Asia. In 1995 the Prime Minister of Singapore, Mr. Goh Chok Tong, took the initiative to organize the first Asia Europe Meeting (ASEM) acting on behalf of the Association of Southeast Asian Nations (ASEAN). After four years it seems that the first stage of 'getting to know each other' has been fulfilled.

This article reviews the first achievements of ASEM and assesses the potential for the second stage. It concludes with some of the outstanding issues, which may be addressed at the ASEM in Seoul in the year 2000.

THREE PILARS OF ASEM

Between 1995 and 1999 the ASEM process has evolved into a multifaceted system of interregional relations based on informality, equality in partnership, and high-level commitment from official leaders and representatives of civic institutions. At the Bangkok Meeting in 1996 ASEM was conceived as a loosely structured biannual meeting between the Heads of State and Government of the fifteen EU member states and ten Asian countries, including seven ASEAN members and China, Japan, and South Korea. Though it was basically an intergovernmental initiative, the European and Asian partners supported various endeavours to ensure that the ASEM process would evolve with substantial contributions from civil society institutions from both regions. A major step in this respect was the first Asia Europe Forum on Culture, Values and Technology of January 1996 in Venice, which was attended by one hundred representatives of educational, cultural, and commercial institutions from all member states and was designed to provide inputs to the Bangkok Meeting.[1]

The 'Chairman's Statement' from Bangkok is the main guiding document for the ASEM process underpinning it with three pillars: one pillar is concerned with fostering political dialogue, one with re-enforcing economic co-operation, and one with promoting co-operation in the social and cultural fields.

This three-pronged approach is what makes the difference between ASEM and the Asia Pacific Economic Co-operation (APEC), the twenty-one member grouping of countries from the Pacific Rim including the US, Canada, Australia, and New Zealand. The former Commissioner for External Relations, RT Hon. Sir Leon Brittan, explained the difference in a speech on Europe-Asia Relations for the International Institute for strategic Studies in London as follows: 'Unlike APEC, ASEM is not confined to economic and commercial matters - although they do play an important part, as is inevitable given that the European Union and its Asian partners in ASEM together make up around half of world GDP - ASEM also includes a cultural and people-to-people dimension and a substantive political dialogue. One of its key features is its informality ....'[2]

In 1997 Asian and European Ministers of Economic and Foreign Affairs met in Japan and Singapore to address each of the three pillars. Expert Group meetings in the areas of trade, investment and finance, and numerous encounters between representatives of the two regions' civic and cultural institutions followed suit to help attune policy approaches, develop joint activities, and put resources and people into the right place.

In the area of political relations, Foreign Affairs MM discussed co-operation in the context of global and regional challenges such as the new multi-polarity of power and potential areas of conflict related, *inter alia*, to the Koreas, Taiwan, the South China Sea, and the crisis in Southeast Europe. The ministers agreed that global problems like terrorism, drug trafficking, and environmental degradation demand global responses, but also stressed the importance of mutually reinforcing regional approaches to these challenges. The global dialogue should be underpinned by discussions on such matters at the regional level to 'highlight and expand common ground, enhance mutual understanding, trust and friendship and promote and deepen co-operation.'[3] ASEM should become a platform from which contributions can be made to global solutions.

Economic co-operation was discussed at the ASEM Economic Affairs MM in Japan under the motto of 'a new comprehensive Asia-Europe Partnership for Greater Growth.' Ministers agreed that Asia and Europe should work together to set priorities, define policies and take measures to promote economic co-operation in ASEM, thereby maximizing inter-regional synergies.[4] They addressed various topics of a technical and proce-dural nature, not least with an eye to developing common positions in the multilateral institutions. Apart from trade liberalization issues *per se*, the agenda included talks on customs co-operation, mutual recognition of industrial standards, protection of industrial or intellectual property rights, criteria for rules of origin and local content, and fine-tuning of taxation and investment regulations.

On the same occasion, the Ministers of Economic Affairs reaffirmed ASEM's commitments to developing the WTO, greater tariff liberalization, and new issues (such as trade and investment, trade and competition policy, transparency in government procurement and other trade facilitation measures). They also proposed to undertake an expeditious review of regional trade agreements and the generalized system of preference (GSP).

Concerning sustainable economic growth, the Ministers agreed that those issues of energy security, environmental protection, and sustainable economic growth were best dealt with as a package and prioritized. Energy deregulation was noted as one important area for co-operation, as was the promotion of technological co-operation and co-operation in the areas of culture and education.

In the area of civic and cultural relations, ASEM supports closer people-to-people links and joint cultural activities, as these are vital to greater mutual understanding between the two regions. For this purpose the Asia Europe Foundation (ASEF) was established in February 1997, to be based in Singapore with a mandate to steer civic aspirations in both regions towards concrete activities aimed at promoting economic integration, improving mutual understanding, and aligning diverse governance systems and political orientations of the two regions.[5]

RELEVANCE OF ASEM IN THE WAKE OF THE CRISIS IN ASIA

When ASEM 2 took place in April 1998 in London, the process had been overtaken by the financial crisis in Asia. Though by June 1997 the EU had already established a range of technical and financial support linkages and was voting in favour of the main multilateral support initiatives, some media on both sides still challenged the relevance of ASEM.

Notwithstanding some criticism from the media, at the London Meeting of 1998 the leaders reaffirmed their pledges of mutual support and addressed the cohesion of the ASEM process and its long-term implications. Representatives of civic institutions from both regions provided inputs at the second Asia Europe Forum on Culture, Values, and Technology in Manila in December 1997.[6] The ASEM leaders adopted an official Co-operation Framework and commissioned an informal Vision Group to set out a course for the long term. In the margins of the Summit, several initiatives were taken by non-governmental organizations addressing questions of civil and political rights and those of economic and cultural rights in both regions.[7]

When the crisis in Asia intensified in the course of 1998, further political and financial support was forthcoming from Europe on top of its huge contributions to IMF and World Bank programmes. In 1998 the EU created a European Network of Financial Expertise (EFEX) to give access to European expertise in the reforming of Asia's financial institutions working in conjunction with Asian experts. An expert working group has been established to deal with mutual trade and investment issues (IEG/SOMTI). Other new policy instruments involving private sector participation include an Investment Promotion Action Plan (IPAP) and a Trade Facilitation Action Plan (TFAP) aimed at reducing non-tariff barriers and technical barriers to trade, an Infrastructure Task Force and regular meetings of Europe Asia Business Councils (EABC).

The ASEM Trust Fund was established at the World Bank and has been operational since June 1998 to provide Asian ASEM partners with money for technical assistance, advice on restructuring their financial sectors and on measures dealing with the growing social problems caused by the crisis. The contribution by the European Commission is around Euro 42 million.

COMPARISON OF EU AND US COMMITMENTS IN ASIA

In January 1999 the European Commission's DG1 for External Relations saw fit to reaffirm the relevance of ASEM and publish an overview of Europe's material and political commitments to Asia, setting these against those of the US.[8]

The figures illustrating the EU's commitments in Asia put the question of relevance into proper perspective. In 1999 European banks have loans outstanding in Asia with a total value of US$365 Billion, compared to US$ 275 held by American banks and US$45 billion held by Japanese banks. [9] Together EU countries account for some 30 per cent of the IMF quota, 27 per cent of the subscribed capital of the World Bank, and 14 per cent of that of the Asian Development Bank. The total value of financial support from Europe to Asia stood at almost Euro 27 billion, which is 18 per cent of the total as compared to an American share of 15 per cent. In 1998 Europe has seen a negative effect on the trade balance with Asia amounting to some Euro 50 billion, compared to US$45 billion cushioned by the US. The figures for overseas development aid and humanitarian aid from the Union to the region triple and double those of the USA. Of the total value of debt relief schemes, the European share was 75 per cent compared with a 10 per cent share for the US. Meanwhile, Europe's paid up share in UN dues is proportionally higher compared with the partly overdue share of the US estimated at US$1.3 billion.

The same overview notes that the EU has lived up to the Trade and Investment Pledge made at the London Summit by sustaining a negative shift in trade balance of around Euro 50 billion in just one year without succumbing to protectionist pressures. The EU has promised that, provided genuine reforms are made in the affected countries, such pressures will not be heeded. And, through the Euro, the EU offers Asian countries the possibility to diversify their debt structure and debt servicing and reduce their vulnerability to fluctuations in the dollar exchange rate. Indeed, given the fact that 85 per cent of stock market transactions and half the world's trade is settled in dollars, the Euro may help to prevent a *de facto* inclusion of Asian countries in the Dollar zone.

EUROPE'S BILATERAL AND INTERREGIONAL PROGRAMMES IN ASIA
The EU also engages in partnerships with a number of Asian countries under bilateral co-operation agreements and with the Association of Southeast Asian Nations under the EU-ASEAN Co-operation Treaty of 1982 and the Joint Co-operation Committee (JCC).[10] Consistent with the objectives of ASEM, these agreements address each of the three main pillars mentioned above without overlooking urgent remedies for the crisis.

In East Asia the EU and Japan are fine-tuning their role in sustaining the region's financial dynamics following the launch of the Miyazawa Fund in 1998 and the introduction of the Euro in January 1999. The EU regards China as a cornerstone in the ASEM process, by supporting China's accession to the WTO and actively engaging each other in the region's political and security problems. With South Korea, the co-operation includes support for financial reform, technology transfer, and educational and young executive exchange programmes.

In the cultural and institutional area initiatives include, *inter alia*, co-operation in tertiary education and legal reform with China, establishment of an EC-China Business Management Institute in Shanghai, and exchange programmes for junior managers, political leaders, and media representatives between the EU these countries.

In the area of EU-ASEAN co-operation, which is seen as a cornerstone in the ASEM process, many initiatives are being undertaken in the context of the JCC, covering the three main pillars defined for the ASEM process. Political issues are addressed through the ASEAN Regional Forum. EU support to democratization and human rights is available for individual countries, notably Indonesia and Cambodia.

Economic co-operation affects *inter alia* support for regional institutions (the ASEAN Secretariat and regional technical agencies), programmes in the area of energy conservation (COGEN), a network for European Business Information Centres (EBICS). Bilateral programmes for Vietnam, Laos, and

Cambodia offer help to these countries to facilitate the transition to a market economy and play a meaningful role in ASEAN, as well as support their future accession to WTO.[11]

Cultural and institutional issues are addressed by means of educational support programmes like the European Studies programmes in Thailand and the Philippines, the establishment of regional centres in applied sciences, and young executive exchange programmes.[12] And region-wide the ASEF organizes people-to-people contacts (Asia Europe Parliamentary contacts, Asia Europe Young leaders Symposiums, the Asia Europe Summer School), and activities in areas of intellectual exchange with support for think tank networking and other meetings covering a variety of topics of mutual interest.

NEW INITIATIVES UNDER THE GERMAN PRESIDENCY

Since early 1999 the signs of stabilization and recovery in Asia are evident, perhaps with the exception of Indonesia. In the first half of that year the German EU presidency was successful in turning the attention of the ASEM leadership back to WTO-related issues in preparation for the New Millennium Round of negotiations. It was also able to focus on the substance of ASEM partnerships with relation to the three pillars at Economic, Foreign, and the Financial MMs with their concomitant technical working arrangements and civic and private sector involvement. On these occasions a broad range of issues in the areas of education, health, welfare, and environment was also addressed in the Asia Europe Co-operation Framework (AECF) and Work Programme.[13] On the initiative of China, a ministerial meeting in the area of Science and Technology Co-operation was added to the ASEM agenda. The year 1999 also saw the inauguration of the Asia-Europe Environmental Technology Centre at Bangkok.

ASEM AND EU SCEPTICISM

The foregoing review of commitments begs the question of why the relevance of ASEM has been questioned so often in the media on both sides. Perhaps this scepticism is the natural outcome of a general feeling that Europe has enough on its hands. Just consider some of the EU's major challenges. The Union is coping with 18 million unemployed workers while upholding the principles of free trade in the face of mounting pressure for market protection. The expansion of the EU by eleven potential new members requires detailed institutional adjustments and is a formidable logistical and human challenge. The EU's contribution to the costs amount to Euro 60 billion compared to an estimated contribution of around US$12 billion from the US.

Add the problem of safeguarding Europe's monetary and fiscal stability with the introduction of the Euro and the necessity of backing up the Euro worldwide. Consider the problem of developing a Common Foreign and Security Policy (CFSP) in view of the instability and reconstruction in Southeast Europe. Likewise, in the area of Justice and Home Affairs huge resources are needed to combat fraud and fend off threats to public safety by criminal organizations.

It also is difficult to define common interests and problems at the regional level because of the heterogeneity of ASEM membership and alternating priorities of European member states holding the six-month presidency of the EU.

In the wake of the recent crisis in Asia and Southeast Europe, the ASEM partners also appear less at ease about upholding the notion of 'equality in partnership.' The upshot can be timidity or a blunt stalemate on sensitive issues, as was the case with the EU's objections to the poor state of human rights and political and civil liberties in Myanmar.

The EU leaders also seem to be handicapped by the reform of the European Commission and the reformulation of the mandate of the European Parliament. Both are necessary institutional adjustments to regain confidence from the general public and dispelling a poor appreciation of Europe's achievements in regional integration by the media.

Perhaps most serious of all is the possibility that because of the absence of a common foreign policy Europe's achievements with integration, no matter how well institutionalized, lack the power of persuasion compared to the power exerted by the US. The EU seems reluctant to promote its essential advantage over the US, which is its capacity for intergovernmental co-operation and building regional institutions across national borders. And, for the sake of maintaining the Transatlantic relationship, Europe appears too timid on issues pertaining to the interests of its Asian partners, particularly those concerning trade liberalization and global security.

A LONG-TERM VISION ON THE ASEM PROCESS

By mid-1999 the Asian-European Vision Group (AEVG) turned out a comprehensive, long-term perspective on the Europe-Asia relationship offering a civic perspective to complement the official one promulgated within the ASEM Co-operation Framework and Work Plan.

The AEVG strongly endorses the idea that Asia-Europe co-operation should be multifaceted, encompassing the main fields of human endeavour. Apart from a range of practical recommendations in each of these areas, the AEVG offers three main *raisons d'être* of ASEM.

45

The first *raison d'être* is ASEM's potential for sharing experiences in regional policy making and institution building gained from the fifty year process of European integration and the thirty year history of regional co-operation of the Association of Southeast Asian nations (ASEAN).

The second *raison d'être* is ASEM's balancing effect in the triangle of economic powers made up by Europe, Asia, and North America in the framework of multilateral institutions such as the IMF, World Bank, WTO, and the UN.

The third *raison d'être* is ASEM's potential for development co-operation with third countries.

The AEVG has drafted nine major recommendations and twenty-one additional ones, which it believes can help create a 'prosperous common living space' in the twenty-first century. The notion of a common prosperity sphere is one for the long-term that assumes a state of fully-fledged integration on the Eurasian continent, in which goods, money, people, and ideas can move around freely.

Liberalization is the key notion in all areas of exchange or common interest such as trade, finance, infrastructure, environment, education, and governance. In addition to setting new rules for engagement, the AEVG envisages ASEM support infrastructures in these areas formed by joint councils and forums and specialized interregional centres, and the provision of ASEM funds to finance selected co-operation activities. In the educational sector for example, the AEVG refers to mutual attuning of educational methods and credits (rules), creating educational forums and centres (infrastructure) and financing scholarship and exchange programmes (activities). Other proposed linking facilities include those on activities managed by ASEF in the cultural and intellectual area, and twinning of urban and local authorities, or one or the other.

In the security area the AEVG recommends the ASEM leadership reaffirm stated commitments to promote good governance, political dialogue, and ratify the International Convenants on Civil and Political Rights and those on Economic, Social, and Cultural Rights. The ASEAN Regional Forum (ARF) and the Organisation for Security Co-operation in Europe (OSCE) may be linked to provide a viable institutional platform. At the operational level the AEVG sees possibilities for establishing Joint Training Centres and undertaking collaborative peacekeeping interventions. In view of the link between social imbalances, poverty, and unemployment and security issues, the AEVG suggests that the ASEM Trust Fund provide the necessary funds.

Finally, the AEVG supports the inclusion of ministerial meetings in the areas of Science and Technology, Education, and Environment. It foresees the accession of new members from South Asia and it suggests that a secretariat may be established to carry the ASEM process through its second phase.

POTENTIAL FOR STRENGTHENING INTERREGIONAL LINKS

As an intergovernmental organisation ASEM includes two major regional organizations, i.e. the EU and ASEAN, and individual Asian countries. There is tremendous scope for elaboration of the regional dimensions of the relationship within the ASEM context.

Before individual countries and their citizens can comply with global regulations and reap the fullest benefits of free trade and universal rights, a certain experience of regional consensus building and improving capacities for intergovernmental co-ordination will be most helpful. Such experience should make countries better able to cope with the domestic implications of a future free trade regime and global civil society. The intergovernmental format of the ASEM grouping is ideally suited to this purpose; building on the experience of the EU and ASEAN with regional policy co-ordination.

In the economic areas that fall within the ambit of the IMF and WTO, the EU's regional experience has resulted in the development of a highly sophisticated executive apparatus. In the area of customs and that of technical and non-tariff barriers to trade, the member states enjoy a harmonized nomenclature and the smooth expeditions of goods in transit, and they can rely on the European standards and conformance system for testing, certification, accreditation and technical regulations.[14] Yet other experience relates to Internal Market (labour, taxation regulations) and Competition (mergers and market access).

Concerning the financial reforms in Asia under the auspices of the IMF and the flawed perceptions of Europe's involvement in these, there is ample opportunity to use European expertise gained with the exchange rate mechanism, the Euro, the European Central Bank, and the European Investment Bank. This would not only reflect the region's financial commitments in Asia, it also allows ASEM partners to benefit from the EU's experience in these matters rather than just offering a carbon copy of IMF recipes.

In the political, cultural and social fields, ASEM may use the EU's experience in ensuring equal rights for all its citizens; programmes aimed at increasing citizens' participation in policy development and the building of democratic institutions. The EU has much to share in terms of its track record in developing cultural and sports exchanges, stimulating university co-operation (including collaborative research and staff or student mobility programmes), and the rehabilitation of disadvantaged regions through 'structural' and/or 'cohesion' funds. Likewise, EU experience may be useful for combating trans-boundary pollution and trans-national crime, the protection of the rights of children, women, minority populations, and providing for the elderly and disabled.[15]

Though primarily concerned with intra-European policies and actions, EU services and agencies also make this expertise available to third countries through the international divisions of respective Directorate-Generals or via the designated DG for External Relations dealing with East Europe (PHARE and TACIS), the Mediterranean countries (MEDA), Latin America (MERCUSOR), and Southeast Asia (ASEAN).

GRADUAL INSTITUTIONAL ALIGNMENT AMONG ASEM MEMBERS
Although the difference between Europe and Asia in terms of regional integration is huge, the potential for gradual institutional alignment is increasing because Asia is moving upwards on the integration scale and Europe is coming down.[16]

On the one hand there is a trend towards more cohesion and integration - and hence institutionalization - amongst Asian nations. Intergovernmental approaches in Asia have reached a high degree of intensity, involving departmental working groups and committees, senior official meetings, ministerial meetings and summit activities, and increasing participation from civil society and private sector associations. The ASEAN experience of thirty years has shown that consensus-based policy making may become obsolescent unless this region proceeds to institutionalized policy making. Asia must adopt further integration measures and install institutional capacity to cope with global regulatory processes in the context of WTO and the UN. Learning first how to cope with the impact of these regulations on a regional basis may help Asian countries to cushion the impact of these rules, and exert influence on the outcome of the next WTO Millennium Round of trade negotiations. Also in order to attract foreign direct investment there is a need for deeper co-operation, as international investors will tend to undertake sourcing and marketing activities region-wide rather than nation-wide, and take their investment decisions accordingly.

Equally in the political and security area there are plenty of good reasons for Asian countries to be mutually engaged, notably to solve lingering disputes on access to contested parts of the South China Sea, to cope with the process of Chinese unification and with China's transition to a socialist market economy and its accession to the WTO, the peacekeeping process in the Korean peninsula, and the maintenance of political stability in parts of Southeast Asia heavily affected by the crisis.

On the European side, meanwhile, there is a trend towards loosening up the highly centralized EU system, which will be impossible to sustain at the present level in view of the accession of eleven new members to the Union, and because of the decreasing popular support for the Union. According to the notions of subsidiairity and proportionality, which were reaffirmed in the Amsterdam Treaty, the Union should evolve according to new divisions of authority and competency at the regional, national, and sub-regional level. And it allows for new forms of regulation based on voluntary agreement rather than regional legislation. The reform of the European Commission by the President, Mr. Prodi, may also be conducive to such alignment by reducing overlap of competencies among EC services and clarifying the distinction between policies and actions among and within those services[17].

The regional dimension in ASEM will also become more important when the competency for external relations will rest solely with the Commissioner For External Relations, the Rt. Hon. Chris Patten, who may benefit from his experience as the former governor of Hong Kong. [18]

Assuming that these trends will persist under the Finnish Presidency and will be on the agenda of the next Intergovernmental Conference, and also assuming that relations within Asia continue to become more institutionalized, the two regions may meet each other halfway within the ASEM context.

POTENTIAL FOR CONCERTED ACTION IN THE MULTILATERAL FRAMEWORK

ASEM has been introduced at a very timely moment in the multilateral framework to present a countervailing force to the US in the drive towards global liberalization. Gerald Segal argued that one of the most important rationales for ASEM is 'to keep the Americans honestly committed to multilateralism.'[19]

Segal refers to the fact that ASEM makes up one of the three base lines of a triangular pattern of links between the world's three core economic regions, East and Southeast Asia, North America and Europe. As such, ASEM is one of three alliances representing the interests of these regions in the multilateral institutions and the global public policy framework. The two other links are those between North America and Asia in the Asia Pacific Co-operation (APEC) and those between North America, Mexico and Europe within an emergent Transatlantic Free Trade Area (TAFTA).

This triangle provides the basic structure for a world order at the beginning of the third millennium. If ASEM becomes more and more settled, Europe and Asia will be able to identify areas of common interest and set priorities for concerted action in the international forums where the rules, regulations, and standards for governing global financial, commercial, political and cultural relations are being determined. Once a CFSP has been developed and is applied in the ASEM context the members can jointly influence the outcome of international negotiations to their mutual interest. At the outset of the third millennium, the point has been reached where the EU should break the shackles of timidity and become a viable countervailing force vis à vis the US in Asia.

ASEM IN THE WTO AND UN TRIANGLE

In the forthcoming Millennium Round of WTO negotiations on the legal ground-rules for international commerce and trade policy (including further liberalization measures and creating impartial mechanisms for settling disputes), ASEM offers an excellent platform for concerted action. In view of the accession requests for future WTO membership by China and non-ASEM member countries (which may be part of an enlarged ASEAN or belong to the group of eleven aspiring EU members), ASEM seems to be a logical interface between regional and global multilateral trading structures.

Meanwhile APEC's attempt to liberalize trade in fifteen economic sectors has failed and was referred back to WTO arbitration. In view of the apparent lack of results in APEC, ASEM may be able to seize the momentum and assume a common stance in the Millennium Round. Otherwise one would have a scenario of 'an inverted domino-theory': one Asian country after another would succumb to rules and standards defined at WTO negotiations in which the US occupies the position of strength and would exert its power on a case by case basis. [20]

The ASEM Heads of State and Government and their ministers and officials may also deal more firmly with institutional questions, like for instance the latest stalemate around the election of the new WTO presidency. According to observers the solution that was imposed by the US was the unsatisfactory compromise of an alternating presidency for three years between New Zealand's candidate, Mr. Micheal Moore, and the Thai Deputy Prime Minister, Mr. Supachai Panitchpakdi. These observers have interpreted this solution as a set-back for developing nations and those of Asia in particular, seeing the liberalization of trade in agricultural products and the liberalization of financial markets as working to the detriment of Asia's populations. [21]

Likewise, there is a great potential for concerted ASEM action in UN institutions, notably those concerned with Conventions on security issues and the ratification of the Conventions on civic and political rights and those on economic and cultural rights. [22]

Following an informal ASEM meeting on human rights and the rule of law held in Sweden, the matter has been taken up directly with China, albeit with mixed results. Commissioner Brittan has commented on this subject: 'The Human Rights Dialogue is our only means of directly and regularly engaging China specifically on these issues. We must not let the dialogue become an empty shell; we should constantly strive for concrete progress.' He added, however, that there is a link with economic progress: 'The economic reform process is possibly the most eye-catching and dramatic aspect of today's China. Reforms primarily geared to strengthening and developing the domestic economy - particularly efforts to establish a predictable and rule-based legal system - are potentially also helpful for the development of human rights. Intuitively, the logic of the market, which requires decentralized decision-making, a stable and predictable legal framework and a well-educated labour force, should promote a more open and plural political system.' [23]

In view of his experience with the transfer of Hong Kong, the Commissioner for External Relations, Mr. Chris Patten, will be well prepared for carrying this issue further with China. The EU-China relationship will be exemplary for the ASEM process as a whole and the Union's approach to human rights issues in Asia in comparison to that of the US will be a crucial test of ASEM's maturity.

ASEM AND GLOBAL CULTURE

In the sphere of global cultural influences the role of ASEM may be less easily defined, taking into account that this area is less clearly attributable to any particular force in the global setting and not yet governed by designated global institutions and bodies. Although there is a general impression of American cultural hegemony at the level of popular culture and mass communication, the reverse is the case when it comes to issues of cultural diversity, heritage, and identities, in which area the ASEM region is keeper of the worlds largest stock.

In any case, the degree of exposure of the populations of ASEM member countries to global cultural influences is still largely uncharted, as are the effects of the same. So far there is no reason to sound the alarm about mankind's inevitable uniformity. Still, ASEM member states (including the EU) are wise to develop concerted actions and play a full and meaningful role in determining the outcome of such processes in the global cultural framework for the present century.

Potential for Joint Links with Third Countries

Concerning the third rationale for ASEM as proposed by the Vision Group, i.e. its potential for joint development co-operation in third countries, this may be premature at the present stage but there certainly is scope for joint action in relation to other regional groupings.

The suggestion by the Vision Group that ASEM should jointly undertake development co-operation in third countries is by no means lacking in sense considering that these countries may benefit from the introduction of Asian solutions. In many developing countries the introduction of European practices is not feasible or touches upon sensitivities deriving from to former colonial links.

In this respect it should be borne in mind that there are diverse perceptions of ASEM in terms of its humanitarian, social, and political rationales, compared to its concerted objectives of strengthening economic and trade links. The latter objective may be seen as the prerogative of private sector entities, rather than that of ASEM agencies. A public sector definition of ASEM may actually be favoured among the social-democratic EU governments, who may find that market liberalization has done enough damage.

Considering the above reservations and qualifications, ASEM initiatives may best be confined to linking up with regional processes in Africa, Latin America, South Asia, Central Asia, and the South Pacific. Given the existing support links of the EU with the Organisation of African States, MERCOSUR, the Andes Pact, the Caribbean Community, the Mediterranean group (MEDA), and the South Asia Association for regional Co-operation (SAARC), ASEM may provide for a suitable venue in which to introduce the combined Asian and European experiences. Likewise, practices that have proven worthwhile in one of the other regional relationships with the EU may be applied in the ASEM context.

Deployment of Civil Society in the ASEM Framework

The ASEM Heads of State and Government are particularly keen to create broad popular appeal for their partnership in order to overcome historical sensitivities and to cushion the more volatile political and economic relationships across regions.

The deployment of civic institutions is a key element in the notion of governance in the ASEM framework. It involves political leaders and parliamentarians, civil engineers and managers, scientists and intellectuals, religious and spiritual leaders, artists and performers, editors and journalists.

EU institutions and European and Asian governments have organized or sponsored various interregional forums, involving hundreds of institutions and individuals from each of the twenty-five ASEM member countries and a number of South Asian ones. The Asia Europe Cultural Forums of Venice and Manila in 1996 and 1997 were the broadest in terms of the topics covered, including technology exchanges, cultural values and religion, governance systems and interregional security issues.[24]

There was general agreement at these forums that there is much common ground between the members of the ASEM grouping in each of these areas. However, to see cultural and educational links under ASEM as a means of achieving interregional convergence can be an illusion or at best a matter for the *longue durée*. Recent events have proven that such efforts may be overtaken by sheer political or economic volatility.

Instead of striving for convergence of European and Asian governance systems and indulging in mind-searching exercises aimed at reaching mutual understanding, it may be more appropriate to strive for minimal compatibility in the various areas with which the ASEM process is concerned. In view of the heterogeneity of members this may imply only partial adjustment of rules, procedures and standards.

Understood in these terms, the representatives of civil society in the ASEM process are expected to make a contribution to what has been defined by Rosenau in 1992 as 'governing without government' in a global setting[25]. Governance then refers to setting up a trans-national system of rules, which is 'endowed with non-formal authority' and 'emerging arrangements concerning the distribution of power, hierarchy and legitimacy.' In this definition, governance is a combination of formal institutions and inter-subjective meanings, including principles, norms, rules, and decision-making procedures. These are shared by the majority of participants who are prepared to give up some degree of autonomy and share some degree of control over the future course of their respective areas of interest.

STRENGTHENING THE THIRD PILLAR

Understanding the ASEM process as a mixture of official and civil relations, means that traditional forms of nation-based or interregional diplomacy are replaced in favour of mixed interregional forums consisting of eminent persons groups, technical task forces, working groups, policy-making committees, think tanks, and civic and cultural institutions.

In the area of security policy co-ordination, such channels for communication have achieved to the illustrious status of 'track-two' diplomacy. But also in more down-to-earth areas of interest, civil participation within the ASEM framework may have the benefit of supplementing or even substituting, the conventional skills, methods and qualifications of government leaders, politicians, and diplomats.

To make sure that this works, civic forces in Asia and Europe must act in conjunction with official forces and address those issues that are also on the agendas of the MMs and the committees and working groups. Or they should make sure that these will be included (i.e. issues pertaining to political, economic, and cultural relations). The temporal logic of the ASEM process as defined in 1996 by Singapore's prime Minister, Goh Chok Tong, should also be taken into account: stage one is getting to know each other, stage two is constructive dialogue, and stage three is consensus-based policy making.[26]

At the present state of the ASEM process, the primary objective of getting to know each other and raising mutual awareness has already been brought a great deal further, if not always in a preconceived way. If we understand the notion of 'constructive dialogue' as 'confidence building' and see this as the main priority at the second stage, the focus should be on jointly monitoring and solving problems in key areas of mutual interest.

Other elements concern the promotion of regional institutional development, student, staff, and executive exchange schemes and collaborative research programmes with the objective of pooling of mutual knowledge resources and sharing proven solutions. In view of the different degrees of regional integration and the unequal endowments across Europe and Asia, confidence-building measures and activities should always be undertaken with an eye to strengthening the regional capacity in Asia and involving the EU's weaker members.

In the area of security, Segal and Dong Ik Shin offer some suggestions for civic and intellectual involvement in confidence-building under ASEM, including the monitoring of cross-regional arms trade interests and strengthening regional security institutions with an eye to establishing a common peace keeping regime.[27] Other suggestions from these authors concern official support for a possible Asia Monetary Fund and an AsiaTom, two measures which would have similar confidence-building effects in the respective areas of trade and finance and energy relations.

In 1998 a combined initiative of Dutch, Danish and Korean origin was launched under the name of PEARL (Programme for Europe-Asia Research Linkages) with the objective of nurturing a shared research culture in these areas of interest.[28]

The convenors of PEARL propose to deploy ASEM's intellectual potential in the area of macro-economic studies, business management, and sustainable development, notably monitoring and preservation of bio-diversity and improving water and soil management. In the socio-cultural area their proposal for intellectual pooling concerns educational development, promotion of the performing arts, and the preservation of cultural heritage, or topics related to public administration and governance, public health, public safety, and labour relations. Though global in nature, these topics are best researched in terms of their cross-boundary or regional implications.

PROSPECTIVE ISSUES FOR THE SEOUL MEETING

In the absence of an ASEM Secretariat the EC DG1 website offers the most comprehensive information on the ASEM process under the heading of bilateral relations.[29] Based on its four key characteristics as an informal, multi-dimensional, and equal partnership backed by regular Summit encounters, the ASEM process has evolved in a large number of ministerial and official meetings, working group and civic encounters, and includes a growing number of interregional institutions.

In view of the Seoul Meeting in 2000, three important issues remain to be solved. One issue concerns the viability of the ASEM process as such. Apart from the Summits, the main guiding mechanisms are the AECF and the Vision Group, the latter representing a civic perspective. However, as the Vision Group has pointed out, media coverage and public awareness are insufficiently underpinning the process, as it is borne mainly by elite constituencies from both regions. The suggestion that an ASEM secretariat be formed may be a solution, but note that similar secretariats of ASEAN and APEC have so far been unable to build broad constituencies. Nor will it be easy for an ASEM Secretariat to avoid a further proliferation of meetings and prevent a sense of forum fatigue.

The second issue concerns the lack of cohesion among the ASEM membership because of the heterogeneity of the Asian participation. There is a similar degree of heterogeneity of the European participation, which will increase after the expansion of the EU. Such heterogeneity may affect the cohesion of the ASEM community negatively. There are different views in the EU on which Asian participants are to be seen as the or a cornerstone (notably China and ASEAN) and how Japan's role should be defined in this context. There are diverging interests among the main European countries, while the EU has to manage its bilateral and multilateral dialogues over and beyond the ASEM process without overlap and contradictions.

The third issue concerns the imbalance in the three main pillars in the ASEM structure. Though the ASEM process is primarily driven by the Foreign Affairs apparatuses of the grouping, political dialogue and cultural and civic relations are treated merely as functional prerequisites for successful economic relations in terms of consensus on issues and mutual understanding of practices. Since public awareness of the ASEM process will depend mainly on the ebb and flow of political and civic-cultural relations it will be difficult to develop public interest and support in this manner.

If, on the contrary, the political and civic-cultural dimensions are treated as important objectives in their own right, a sense of long-term confidence could emerge under which public support will be forthcoming and the conditions for thriving economic relations between Asia and Europe will be put into place.

NOTES

*   First published in He Fang Cuan and Ulrich Niemann Asia and Europe - towards a better mutual understanding. Second ASEF Summer School Beijing, China, 22 August - 5 September, Singapore, ASEF 2000, pp. 105-120. See also webside http://www.asef.org/sources/ index.html.

1   Re.: The Message from Venice, 18-19 January 1996. (with support from Dg1b, External Economic Relations, Asia Directorate, under former Commissioner Manuel Marin and Dg1a External Relations East Asia under former Commissioner Sir Leon Brittan.

2   Re.: http://europa.eu/int/comm/dg01/1203slb.htm Europe/Asia Relations Speech by the Rt. Hon. Sir Leon Brittan QC, Vice-President of the European Commission, International Institute for Strategic Studies - London, 12 March 1999.

3   Re.: Declaration from the First ASEM Foreign Ministers' Meeting, Singapore, 15 February 1997.

4   Re.: Declaration from the First ASEM Economic Ministers Meeting, Tokyo, 19 September 1997; principles agreed upon included:
    a. Common commitment to market economy and to necessary reform; b. Closer co-operation and dialogue between government and the business sector, with the business sector as the engine of growth; c. Non-discriminatory liberalisation, transparency and open regionalism; d. Consistency and compliance with applicable international rules, particularly those of the WTO; and e. Mutual respect and equal partnership, with recognition of the economic diversity within and between Asia and Europe.

5   Re.: the Asia-Europe Foundation Ministerial Declaration, Singapore, 15 February 1997: to promote exchanges between think-tanks, people and cultural groups.'

6   Re: The Message from Manila, 10-12 December 1997.

7   Re.: Council for Asia-Europe Co-operation, CAEC; re.: the Alternative
     ASEM, Institute for International Relations (UK) and the Transnational
     Institute (NL).
8   Re.: http://www.europa.eu/dg01a Asian Economic Crisis: EU-US
     burden sharing. Update with January-September 98 trade data. Dg I
     External Relations, Brussels March 1999.
9   Re.: Brian Bridges 'Europe and the Asian Financial Crisis' in *Asian
     Survey* XXXIX/3, May/June 1999, Berkeley, University of California.
10   Re.: http://www.europa.eu/dg01b (in May 1999 the 13th JCC took
     place after delay caused by the joining of Myanmar to ASEAN, the
     1982 Treaty concerns only the original ASEAN members).
11   Re.: EC Bangkok Delegation on a 1.40 million euro (US$1.47 million)
     training programme for Cambodian officials in a range of topics,
     including international law, negotiation skills, trade and economic
     policy to develop the skills necessary to play a full and active role in
     the ASEAN integration process. The EU is one of Cambodia's main aid
     donors and has given more than 265 million euros in grant aid since
     1992, Reuters 28 July 1999.
12   Including European Studies Programmes in Thailand and the
     Philippines, linking European University Network with the ASEAN
     University Network, and the Junior Executive Exchange Programme
     (JEM).
13   Re.: http://europa.eu.int/comm/dg01/asemproc.htam The ASEM Pro-
     cess. AEFC, Work Programme and Vision Group. Re.: http://www.aus-
     waertiges-amt.de. ASEM-Aussenministertreffen am 29 März 1999,
     referring to a Ban on Biological and Toxic weapons; Reconfirmation of
     the UN Charters and Vienna Declaration of 1993; issues of inter-
     national crime, drugs, child and gender related violence, education,
     poverty alleviation, climate change.
14   Including bodies such as CEN, CENELEC and ETSI, in the areas of
     industrial co-operation (Eureka and Esprit, Airbus), information and
     statistics, (Eur-op and Eurostat).
15   Including education (Erasmus and Socrates), research and technology
     (Fifth Framework Programme and Joint Research Centre), environment
     (European Environment Agency), cultural co-operation (Community
     Framework Programme 2000).
16   Re.: Leo Schmit 'Reflections from the ASEM Bowl in China', in *IIAS
     Newsletter* 20, IIAS, Leiden 1999. This assumption was challenged by
     the Asian and European students attending the 2nd ASEF Summer
     School but has later been vindicated by the ASEAN plus 3 initiative.
17   Re.: http://europa.wu.int/comm/mewcomm/pr_en.htm

Speech by Romano Prodi, President Designate of the European Commission, to the European Parliament, 21 July 1999, Straatsburg/Brussels.

18 http://europa.eu.int/comm. The new organisation of the European Commission, July 1999 Brussels.

19 Re.: G. Segal, 'Thinking strategically about ASEM: the subsidiarity question', in *The Pacific Review* 10/1, 1997, pp. 124-34.

20 Re.: note 16 Concerning this point I was accused by a Mr. P. Nyri of using an inappropriate and alarming anti-american tone, applying Machiavellian reasoning and united front discourse in a Letter to the Editor in *IIAS Newsletter* 21. However, I still stand by it.

21 Re.: Walden Bello The WTO's Big Losers', in Far Eastern Economic Review June 24 1999, Hong Kong; re.: G. Pierre Goad 'The U.S. flops on Free Trade' *Far Eastern Economic Review* 15 July 1999, Hong Kong.

22 Re.: Convention Against Torture and Other Cruel Inhuman or Degrading Treatment or Punishment.
Convention on the Elimination of All Forms of Discrimination against Women; Convention on the Rights of the Child; International Convention on the Elimination of All Forms of Racial Discrimination; International Convention on the Protection of the Rights of All Migrant Workers and Members of Their Families; International Covenant on Civil and Political Rights; International Covenant on Economic, Social and Cultural Rights; Optional Protocol to the International Covenant on Civil and Political Rights Second Optional Protocol to the International Covenant on Civil and Political Rights.

23 Re.: note 3.

24 Re.: 'Message of Venice' (January 1996) and 'Message of Manila '(December 1997); Re.: L.Th. Schmit and P. v.d. Velde 'Asia Europe Forum on Culture, Values and Technology, towards a stronger mutual understanding' in *IIAS Newsletter* 7 Re. L.Th. Schmit, 'Deployment of knowledge and science between Europe and Southeast Asia;' in *IIAS Newsletter* 9, 1996.

25 Re.: J. Rosenau, *Governance without government: order and change in world politics*. Cambridge University Press 1992 (co-editor E-O Czempiel).

26 Re.: Goh Chok Tong 'The Asia Europe Dialogue' in P. van der Velde (ed.) *Cultural rapprochement between Asia and Europe. Five essays on the Asia-Europe relationship*, Leiden, IIAS (1997).

27 Re.: Dong-Ik Shin and G. Segal 'Getting serious about Asia-Europe security co-operation' in Wim Stokhof and Paul van der Velde *ASEM:*

A Window of Opportunity. London and New York: Kegan Paul International and Leiden and Amsterdam: IIAS, 1999.

28 Re.: R. Cribb, 'Pearl Workshop. Asia-Europe research strategies for the 21st century' Yonsei University Seoul, IIAS Leiden, NIAS Copenhagen, 7-9 October 1998, in *IIAS Newsletter* 18, February 1999, Re.: W. Stokhof 'Bringing the communities together. What more can be done?' in Wim Stokhof and Paul van der Velde ASEM *A Window of Opportunity*. London and New York: Kegan Paul International and Leiden and Amsterdam: IIAS, 1999.

29 Re.: http://europa.eu.int/comm/dg01/asemproc.htm.

CHAPTER 6

ASEM - TRANSREGIONAL FORUM AT THE CROSSROADS

JÜRGEN RÜLAND

Influential studies have portrayed globalization as a new stage in the process of modernization. Ulrich Beck, a leading German sociologist, links globalization to the concept of a 'second modernity'. The latter is distinguished from the 'first modernity' which Beck associates with the rise of the nation state (national revolution) and industrialization (industrial revolution) (Beck, 1997:115-19). If differentiation of social roles and functions, division of labour and rationalization of resources (Schwengel, 1999:12) may be taken as salient elements of modernization, then economic globalization has also contributed to a marked change in the international order. It has been the driving force behind a growing functional and spatial differentiation of international relations. Over the last thirty years a persistently deepening and increasingly complex multilevel international system has emerged, which is organizing relations within the Triad (North America, Western Europe, East and Southeast Asia) and gradually integrating the peripheries of the latter into the core regions of the world economy.

THE DIFFERENTIATION OF INTERNATIONAL RELATIONS

Global multilateral organizations as the apex of this multilevel system evolved first. Some, such as the defunct League of Nations, date back as far as the inter-War period. Their number increased in the post-World War II era - spearheaded by the UN system and the Bretton Woods regimes on trade (GATT) and finance (IMF). Since then, more global regimes have emerged such as those based on maritime resources, outer space, arms control, nonproliferation, to name just a few (Müller, 1993).

Regional organizations began to emerge in the 1950s - with the EEC as frontrunner and model for others in Latin America and, to a lesser extent, Africa, Asia and the Middle East. Yet, this first wave of regionalism was short-lived. In the wake of the turbulences caused by the collapse of the Bretton Woods monetary regime in the early 1970s, the oil crises, and the Latin American debt crisis, many non-European regional organizations disintegrated or fell into a state of paralysis. Yet, since the mid-1980s, regional organizations have begun to proliferate again. This *New Regionalism* has markedly changed the international order. It has revived dormant organizations, deepened existing ones, and given rise to new regional organizations in regions which hitherto have been 'regions without regionalism'.

Contrary to the so-called stumbling bloc hypothesis, the *New Regionalism* was basically an 'open regionalism' and thus not a counter-vailing, but rather a complementary process to globalization (Wyatt-Walter, 1995; Schirm, 1997; Roloff, 1998; Hänggi, 1999). It was a defensive response by nation states to battling the challenges of globally operating, transnational economic actors (such as TNCs and hedge funds), 'complex interdependence' (Keohane/Nye, 1989), and the border-crossing pathologies of globalization by preparing the ground for closer co-operation through the pooling of sovereignty and resources.[1] Regional co-operation thus became a device for mustering bargaining power in international forums, increasing member countries' competitiveness in the global race for export markets, capital, and technologies, and preserving the nation state's steering capacity within its own territory.

With the proliferation and growth of regional organizations, the latter became players in their own right. As a result, interregional bloc-to-bloc relations (such as EU-ASEAN, EU-Mercosur, ASEAN-Mercosur, and so forth) and transregional forums (such as ASEM, APEC, IOR-ARC, Euro-Latin America Summit, Euro-Africa Summit) have assumed intermediary roles between the regional and the global policy level. Sub-regional organizations act as intermediaries at the lower end of the international system. They establish links between regional organizations and their neighbours, serve as preparatory regimes for accession candidates, and act as brackets between the member states of regional organizations, facilitating their integration by transcending the dividing nature of borders. The Euro-regions and European sub-regional co-operation are cases in point (Hrbek/Weyand, 1994). Subregional, border-crossing co-operation can also be found in ASEAN, ECO, and SAARC.

ASEM AND THE RISE OF TRANSREGIONALISM

Depending on the theoretical perspective, transregional forums may be regarded as adopting several functions. They act as balancers, institution builders, rationalizers of global multilateral organizations, and identity builders (Rüland, 1996, 1999; Dieter, 1996; Maull, 1997; Maull/Tanaka, 1997). These functions matter when ASEM's performance as a transregional forum is to be assessed - more than the progress of the somewhat odd assortment of projects agreed on at ASEM 1 in Bangkok (1996).[2]

Transregional forums are performing balancing functions in the search for an equilibrium within the Triad (Roloff, 1998). Accordingly, ASEM and APEC may be interpreted as a coalition of two components of the Triad directed against the third (Hänggi, 1999:70).[3] They allow Triad players to pool bargaining power and to respond to gravitational shifts in world politics and the world economy. And indeed, the genesis and evolution of ASEM shows that - like in the case of APEC - its role as a balancer has been a major *raison d'être* of the forum. ASEM has assumed the role of a vehicle for Europeans to balance the rise of a Pacific economic, and eventually, political zone of gravity (Dent, 1997-8:495). Asians, for their part, have sought to balance what they perceived as an increasingly dominant role of the US in Pacific Asia and a rejuvenation of the Trans-Atlantic co-operation under the Trans-Atlantic Agenda, including the spectre of a TAFTA.

As transregional forums constitute the framework of a trilateral concert of regions (Roloff, 1998; Hänggi, 1999), they follow a basically realist agenda. Yet, inter- and transregional relations based mainly on power do not coincide well with institutionalist and liberal paradigms of international relations. Integration theorists have thus repeatedly warned that regional blocs formed primarily for pooling power do not differ markedly from the behaviour of nation states (Mitrany, 1943). Certainly, there would be fewer and larger players, yet the anarchy of nation states would merely be shifted to a higher plane. The anarchy of nation states would be substituted by an anarchy of regional blocs.

Inter- and transregional forums primarily performing balancing functions lack a long-term perspective. They constitute short-term alliances which are formed in response to a given configuration of international relations. With every structural change in the international system, the rationale for an existing alliance is waning. As a consequence, co-operation loses priority and urgency. If co-operative institutions have been built at all under these conditions, they tend to contract. More often than not, co-operation based on balancing designs does not facilitate deep institutionalization. In fact, this type of loose and informal co-operation has been a major feature of the *'Asian Way'* which - not surprisingly - in many ways adheres to an outdated concept of national sovereignty.

ASEM clearly reflects these dangers of shallow institutionalization corresponding with balancing functions. It is hardly deniable that - at least for Europeans - it seems to have lost in priority in the aftermath of the Asian crisis which has changed the international power equation in favour of the West. Though Europeans made sizeable contributions to the rescue packages put together by international financial institutions, they preferred to work individually through global organizations such as the IMF and the World Bank. ASEM, as an institution, has mainly confined itself to declaratory politics. The only exception was the formation of a trust fund under tutelage of the World Bank, which was set up for reforming the ailing banking system and studying the establishment of social security networks in crisis-stricken states.

More seriously, Asia's economic decline was a source of thinly veiled *schadenfreude* for those Europeans who felt offended by what they viewed as the hubris of Asianists in the boom years prior to the crisis. They became advocates of scaling down the priority of Europe's Asia policy and of exerting presssure on Asian governments to fight corruption, nepotism, and other societal ills which they regarded as the dark side of Asian values and thus the real causes of the financial crisis. Indeed, as preliminary empirical data suggest, Asia seems to have taken a back seat in the foreign policy of major European powers in the post-crisis years.[4] For instance, if we take the frequency of high-level government contacts as an indicator, data for Germany show a decline of interactions at the head of government and foreign minister's level after 1997 (see Table 1).

Table 1 Exchange of High Level Visits, Heads of Government and Foreign Ministers (Source: German Ministry of Foreign Affairs)

Year	German Chancellor's Visits to Asia	German Foreign Minister's Visits to Asia	Asian Heads of Govern-ment Visiting Germany	Asian foreign Ministers Visiting Germany
1989	---	1	---	3
1990	---	---	2	4
1991	---	2	---	2
1992	---	1[b]	2	3[c]
1993	7	2[b]	3[c]	3
1994	---	---	5	2[d]
1995	3	2	1	1
1996	4[a]	3[b]	---	---
1997	2	5[b]	---	3
1998	---	---	2	---

a) Includes attendance of ASEM 1 (1996); b) Includes attendance of G 7 (1993), ASEM 1 (1996) and ASEAN-EU Meeting in Manilla (1992) and Singapore (1997); c) Includes G 7 (1992); d) Includes ASEAN-EU Meeting in Karlsruhe (1994).

For its part, Asia also seems the have adjusted foreign policy priorities and shifted attention to the US, conscient of the latter's dominant role in the IMF and the strategic importance of the North American market for Asia's economic recovery.

While all this suggests that balancing does not provide fertile ground for deep institutionalization - we will nevertheless have to probe into ASEM's role an as institutionaliser. To this end, we may examine ASEM's contribution to institution-building at three levels: The global, trans-regional and the regional level. As far as ASEM has succeeded in establishing a missing link in Triad relations, it has undoubtedly contributed to institution-building at the global level. It has filled a gap in the fledgling network of transregional relations.

Through ASEM a more co-ordinated consultation and, to a lesser extent, co-operation process has been fostered between Asia and Europe. Summits have been institutionalized, there are regular meetings of the foreign, economic, and financial ministers, and - if the Vision Group's report is endorsed by the Third Summit in Seoul - meetings of the ministers in charge of environment, energy, education, and technology will follow, the frequency of senior officials, business delegates and scholars has markedly increased, and there are caucuses on both sides to prepare the meetings (Soesastro/Nuttall, 1997; Rüland, 1999; Bersick, 1999a; Haenggi, 2000). But a co-ordinative mechanism such as a secretariat is still missing. Although the London Summit (1998) formally approved an Asia-Europe Co-operation Framework (AECF) which may be considered as an agreement on the norms of co-operation (Hund, 1998:99-102), a more legally binding, rule setting out the nature of activities is still lacking. Particularly in areas of high politics (such as security, nonproliferation, UN reform and so forth.) ASEM still contents itself with vague declarations. Hence, although a process of creeping institutionalization of ASEM cannot be denied (Lim, 2000), it must still be considered as an informal, consultative, and basically non-binding process (Roloff, 2000).

Undeniably, at least for the short run, ASEM has heightened awareness of both sides for each other and given rise to deliberate efforts to overcome mutually persisting stereotypes. Especially the Asia-Europe Foundation (ASEF) has been spearheading efforts to create a better understanding of the values, traditions, culture, and history of either side. Even more important is ASEF's determined bid to reach beyond the world of officialdom and epistemic communities which are the key promoters of ASEM. ASEF places great emphasis on people-to-people contacts and the involvement of civil society, thereby helping to place Asia-European relations on a broader societal foundation.[5]

At a regional level, ASEM has had institution-building effects on the Asian side. In order to enhance bargaining power and to close ranks, the Asian camp has had to develop co-ordinative mechanisms that match the superior and well-oiled co-ordination machinery of the EU (Soesastro/Nuttall, 1997; Synnott, 1999; Haenggi, 2000). Moreover, ASEM has helped to inaugurate a *de facto* institutionalization of Malaysian Prime Minister Mahathir's controversial East Asian Economic Caucus (EAEC). ASEM and, after for years reciting the Western decline mantra, the sudden reappearance of Western economic prowess and Western hegemony over international organizations during the Asian financial crisis, have become driving forces for closer East and Southeast Asian co-operation. They have taught Asian governments the painful lesson that existing regional co-operation arrangements do not provide them with sufficient bargaining power. In 1997, the first East Asian Summit was held in Kuala Lumpur, since then known as the ASEAN+3 process. Since then, ASEAN+3 has developed its own ministerial rounds, proposed a Vision Group and intensified mutual consultations. One highlight in this respect was ASEAN's most recent Informal Summit in Manila which ended with a joint statement of East and Southeast Asian summiteers, pledging closer economic, monetary, and financial co-operation as well as efforts to intensify 'co-ordination and co-operation in various international and regional fora such as the UN, WTO, APEC, ASEM and ARF.'[6]

Ineluctably, East Asian co-operation has its limits. Most governments stubbornly cling to an outdated concept of national sovereignty. ASEAN, for instance, despite an intensifying, sometimes even acrimonious debate, has not parted company with the sacred cow of non-interference. The details specifying the operation of the recently installed ASEAN High Council, the financial early-warning mechanism and the *troika* cannot be considerd a major deviation from the age-honoured *ASEAN Way*.[7] In fact, both the *Hanoi Declaration* of December 1998 and the 32rd AMM in Singapore have confirmed the traditional value kit of ASEAN co-operation. Therefore it is not far-fetched to conclude that East and Southeast Asian co-operation primarily serves the objective of balancing the West. This reading of Asian co-operation is further corroborated by proposals such as the formation of a *Big Asia Five* consisting of China, India, Japan, Indonesia and South Korea. Indonesian president Abdurrahman Wahid, has been cultivating this idea in an attempt to create a powerful Asian bloc with great bargaining power in global international forums.[8] However, in the light of the thinly veiled rivalry of these nations and their diverse interests, such a bloc does not promise to develop into more than a precarious *ad hoc* alliance when the need arises.

Another question is how far ASEM has been able to play the role of a rationaliser and agenda-setter for global organizations. This function has gained increasing currency in the light of a proliferation of actors in international forums and an increasing complexity in policy matters. If transregional fora serve as clearing houses of interests between the components of the Triad before they enter global forums, they may help avoiding bottlenecks at the apex of the international system. As far as they facilitate processes of global governance, they are strengthening the efficiency and, hence, legitimacy of international organizations and regimes.

Viewed in this light, ASEM's achievements are modest at best. To a limited extent, and without noteworthy success, the forum sought to co-ordinate Euro-Asian positions for the 1996 WTO ministerial meeting in Singapore. The Euro-Asian compromise which agreed to transfer the social standards issue to the ILO (Hund, 1998:92-3) was only temporary and the issue reappeared on the WTO agenda at the inconclusive ministerial meeting in Seattle in December 1999. Europeans also backtracked in their support for the Asian candidate for the WTO chairmanship, Supachai Panichpakdi.[9] Even worse, ASEM utterly failed - as, by the way, did APEC - in the preparations for the 1999 WTO ministerial meeting in Seattle.[10] Yet, the Asia-Europe Co-operation Framework (AECF) and the report of ASEM's Vision group open up avenues for such clearing house activities in the area of UN reform, non-proliferation, environmental, and energy policies. To what extent a convergence of positions in these areas will be achieved at the Seoul Summit will tell us much about the long-term viability of ASEM.

Finally, identity-building functions have rightly been attached to ASEM (Haenggi, 2000). However, identity-building have occurred primarily on the Asian side. Here, ASEM has indeed helped to construct the notion of an East and Southeast Asian region with a set of imagined common cultural values and a core of shared interests. The institution-building processes that have been inspired by and at the same time have driven identity-building have already been analysed earlier. The problem is that, not much identity-building has occurred transcending the two blocs in the sense of an Asian-European axis. On this count, the parallel Asia-Europe NGO Summits seem to have been more successful. What may have been a negative effect emanating on European identity from ASEM as the moratorium on new members has been increasingly frustrating Eastern European countries. Slow accession to the EU and failure to become members of major international forums in which the EU is already represented may kindle feelings of discrimination and neglect.

Yet, identity-building does not necessarily aid deep institutionalization of transregional and regional organizations. It may - as the Asian case shows - also strengthen realist notions of international relations. So far Asian identity building has not been overly successful in overcoming the deep-seated differences between the region's major powers.

WHITHER ASEM TASKS AHEAD

ASEM's future does not so much hinge on the implementation of a basket-full of low politics projects such as these agreed by ASEM 1 in Bangkok, ASEM 2 in London, and outlined in the Vision Group's report. Of course, the Investment Promotion Action Plan (IPAP) the Trade Facilitation Action Plan (TFAP), the Asia-Europe Environmental Technology Centre opened in Bangkok in 1999, and the establishment of an Asia-Europe Business Forum (AEBF) have all been useful projects, intensifying Asian-European relations. But in the long run, ASEM's success will have to be gauged by the extent to which it performs its functions as institutionalizer, rationaliser and agenda-setter for global organizations. In order to achieve this objective, two major conditions must be fulfilled.

As international organizations rely on negotiated and binding agreements, ASEM can only perform its functions as rationalizer and agenda-setter, if its consultations are more achievement-oriented and obtain a more binding character. In fact, the Asian financial crisis has illustrated the vulnerabilities of informal co-operation arrangements. As co-operation is always subjected to severe strains in times of crisis, such a danger is even menacing in loosely organized forums. Non-binding informal agreements are an open invitation to exit behavior of panicking members which, in their desperate efforts to keep costs of crisis management affordable and to evade the domino effects of crisis, prefer to resort to unilateral self-help strategies. It does not need much imagination to see that under these conditions co-operation will be threatened by collapse.

Instead of contenting itself with the present process of creeping institutionalization, ASEM should head towards faster institutionalization. This would include the creation of its own secretariat, permanent working groups in key areas of co-operation, and a more determined bid to move into high politics. Here, ASEM should end bracketing issues which are deemed controversial. By comparison, neither ASEAN nor APEC have an impressive record for solving problems long swept under the carpet. However, if ASEM does not develop a sense of achievement-orientation, it will have to contend with an erosion of interest of European governments and publics. As the latter are strongly influenced by the mass media and the media tend to pay attention only to international events that transcend the threshold of technical and seemingly boring matters of low politics, clearly noticeable progress in key policy areas is a prime condition for ASEM's support by the public and political leaders.

If ASEM's success hinges on institutionalization and a more contractual, legalistic approach, the moratorium on the accession of new members should be maintained. This would perpetuate the numerically asymmetrical composition of ASEM, but as the Asian side has the first entitlement to nominate new members, any enlargement will confront ASEM with new sets of problems that may severely undermine the consolidation of the flegdling forum. With notorious human rights violators such as Burma waiting in the wings, enlargement would not only strain relations among Asian, especially ASEAN, members but also block further progress to ASEM's institutional growth as European consent for an accession of Burma would be elusive.[11] Moreover, while India and Pakistan admittedly are important Asian powers, which should be more engaged through integration into cooperative networks, they would burden ASEM with their bilateral problems and the nuclear proliferation issue.

The second major task ahead is democratization. Multilevel international diplomacy has increasingly mutated into an arcane negotiation process dominated by technical experts and government officials. The protests surrounding the WTO ministerial meeting in Seattle in November 1999 for the first time fully exposed the extent of frustration among those who primarily view international forums as expedient and intransparent facilitators of a neo-liberal globalization agenda. In fact, except for business-related interest groups, neither organizations of civil society nor parliamentarians had a noteworthy role in the preparation of ASEM meetings, or in controlling the policies that the latter agreed on. Perhaps even more serious is the fact that, as Bersick notes, the Vision Group determined procedures of NGO and civil society involvement in the ASEM process, but not one NGO representative sat on this panel (Bersick 1999:10). The attachment of NGOs to ASEF means that they remain relegated to an indirect role in ASEM's decision-making.

Admittedly, it is extremely difficult to find legitimate ways to involve civil society in ASEM. Many advocates of peoples' interests such as the ASEM People's Forum are self-styled representatives of civil society with no legitimately established mandate. Even the invitation issued to national NGO umbrella organizations to attend ASEM meetings is debatable, as the NGO scene is highly fragmented and subjected to fierce internal rivalries. A closer look at the signatories of the People's Vision clearly illustrates these problems. Almost 14 per cent of the signatories came from non-ASEM countries such as the US, Australia, New Zealand, Canada, Fiji, and so forth. Even worse is the fact that several smaller countries were strongly overrepresented, while major powers such as Germany, Italy, Spain, Japan, China, and Indonesia were represented only very weakly or not at all (see Table 2).

Table 2: Origin of Signatories of ASEM People's Vision

Country	NGO Networks	Other Signatories	Total
South Korea	---	26	26
United Kingdom[a]	5	20	25
Ireland	1	23	24
Philippines	---	21	21
Netherlands	---	20	20
Belgium	7	4	11
France	---	8	8
Australia	2	5	7
Germany	---	4	4
USA	---	4	4
Thailand[a]	2	1	3
Canada	1	1	2
Fiji	1	1	2
Italy	---	2	2
Portugal	---	2	2
Brazil	---	2	2
Others[b]	4	6	10
Total	23	150	173

a) Headquarters in UK and in Thailand
b) Includes networks from Vatican City, Austria, Finland and India and other signatories from Cambodia, Norway, New Zealand, Peru, Switzerland and Indonesia.
Source: Asia-Europe People's Forum, A People's Vision towards a more Just, Equal and Sustainable World, List of Signatories (Internet, http://www.tni.org/asia/asem/aepf2.htm)

Yet, the parallel and largely unrelated process of discussing issues in the ASEM's official forums, NGO bodies, and parliaments must be overcome. A temporary, albeit democratically still unsatisfactory, solution could be a corporatist approach which brings together government, business, NGOs as well as parliamentary representatives in the same meetings - preparatory meetings as well as official ASEM meetings. This perhaps could also promote regional activities of Asian and - especially ASEAN - parliaments and would boost the repeatedly aired idea of an ASEAN parliament. If the latter could be facilitated through ASEM, it would definitely be a major contribution by the forum to a deepening of ASEAN institutions and democratization and, hence, of identity-building in Southeast Asia.

Yet, all this is easier said than done. It is more than questionable that all Asian governments would agree to 'Peopling ASEM' (Asia-Europe People's Forum 1998). Beijing, for instance, would probably rather opt out of ASEM rather than allowing NGO representatives to sit on summit and other official meetings. Yet, the parallel NGO network has already gone much farther than the governments when it comes to the development of a common Euro-Asian identity. It rests on agreement in areas that have so far been bracketed by governments. Among them are senstive issues such as human rights, democracy, workers' rights, child labour and the arms trade. In the light of increasing networking among NGOs, failure to establish better co-ordinated co-operation between the official track one and civil society, the violent protests accompanying the WTO ministerial meeting in Seattle may have foreshadowed only more violent confrontations on the sidelines of future ASEM, APEC, WTO, and G 7/8 summits.

NOTES

1 Such as migration, environmental problems, drug trafficking and international terrorism, to name just a few.
2 The Chairman's Statement named the following: an Asia-Europe Investment Promotion Plan, a Trade Facilitation Action Plan, an Asia-Europe Environmental Technology Centre, an Asia-Europe Foundation, an Asia-Europe University Programme, intellectual exchanges, youth exchanges, an Asia-Europe Cooperation Framework, cooperation among customs authorities and development of the Mekong Basin.
3 Not the case for the Euro-Africa Summit and the Euro-Latin America Summit.
4 See Sven Hansen, Das erste Jahr rot-grüner Asienpolitik: Bilanz und Perspektiven, (Internet (http://www.asienhaus.de/eurasien/hansen.htm); and *The Nation Review*, 11 May 1999 (Internet).
5 See Asia-Europe Foundation, Annual Report 1998-1999, Singapore.
6 See Joint Statement on East Asia Cooperation, 28 November 1999 (Internet, http://www.aseansc.org/summit/inf3rd/js_eac.htm).
7 See *The Nation Review*, 27 July 1999 (Internet).
8 See *The Jakarta Post*, 3 December 1999 (Internet).
9 Communication at the Seminar in Brussels, 3 April 2000.
10 The contribution of ASEM to a Milenium trade liberalization round is discussed by Lee (1999).

11 As the wisdom of Burma's accession to ASEAN is increasingly questioned among Asian foreign policy experts, scholars and, privately, even politicians, a nomination of Burma for ASEM membership would also meet the opposition of those ASEAN countries which in the wake of the Asian crisis are interested in better relations to the West.

REFERENCES

Acharya, Amitav (1997) 'Ideas, Identity, and Institution-Building: From the "ASEAN Way" to the "Asia-Pacific Way",' *The Pacific Review*, Vol. 10, No. 3, 1997, pp. 319-346.

--(1998) 'Culture, Security, Multilateralism: The "ASEAN" Way and Regional Order,*Contemporary Security Policy*, No. 1, pp. 55-84.

--(1999) 'Realism, Institutionalism and the Asian Economic Crisis,' in: *Contemporary Southeast Asia*, Vol. 21, No. 1, pp. 1-19.

Asia-Europe Vision Group (1999) For a Better Tomorrow: Asia-Europe Partnership in the 21st Century.

Baumann, Michael (1999) *Verpatzte Verhandlungsrunde in Seattle -- ein Hoffnungszeichen*. Berlin: Germanwatch.

--(1997) *Was heißt Globalisierung?Irrtümer des Globalismus - Antworten auf Globalisierung*. Frankfurt am Main: Suhrkamp Verlag, Edition zweite Moderne.

--(1998) 'Das Demokratie-Dilemma im Zeitalter der Globalisierung,' *Aus Politik und Zeitgeschichte*, B 38/98, 11. September 1998, S. 3-11.

Bersick, Sebastian (1999a) *ASEM: Eine neue Qualität der Kooperation zwischen Europa und Asien*. Münster: LIT-Verlag.

--(1999b) Interkultureller Dialog: Menschenrechts-NGOs zwischen Europa und Asien. Paper präsentiert auf der Jahreskonferenz der Hessischen Stiftung für Friedens- und Konfliktforschung 1999, Vergesellschaftung der Staatenwelt? Der Einfluß von Nichtregierungsorganisationen auf Sicherheit und Herrschaft.

Bowles, Paul (1997) 'ASEAN, AFTA and the New Regionalism,' *Pacific Affairs*, Vol. 70, No. 2, Summer, pp. 219-34.

Busse, Nikolas and Hanns W. Maull (1999) 'Enhancing Security in the Asia-Pacific. European Lessons for the ASEAN Regional Forum,' *Internationale Politik und Gesellschaft*, No. 3, pp. 227-36.

Dent, Christopher M. (1997-8) 'The ASEM: Managing the New Framework of the EU's Economic Relations with East Asia,' *Pacific Affairs*, Vol. 70, No. 4, pp. 495-516.

Dieter, Heribert (1996) 'Regional Trade Blocs: A Help or a Hindrance to the WTO?,' *Asia Times*, 19 August 1996, p. 8.

--(1998) *Die Asienkrise. Ursachen, Konsequenzen und die Rolle des Internationalen Währungsfonds*. Marburg: Metropolis Verlag.

European Institute for Asian Studies (1998) *The Role of the EU in Southeast Asia: A Political, Economic and Strategic Review*, Luxembourg.

Hänggi, Heiner (1999) 'ASEM and the Construction of the New Triad,' *Journal of the Asia Pacific Economy*, Vol. 4, No. 1, pp. 56-80.

Haenggi, Heiner (2000) Regionalism through Interregionalism: East Asia in ASEM, mimeographed paper.

Hansen, Sven (1999) Das erste Jahr rot-grüner Asienpolitik: Bilanz und Perspektiven, (Internet (http://www.asienhaus.de/eurasien/hansen.htm);

Henderson, Callum (1998) *Asia Falling? Making Sense of the Asian Currency Crisis and Ist Aftermath*. Singapore: McGraw-Hill Book Co.

Higgott, Richard (1994) 'Ideas, Identity and Policy Coordination in the Asia-Pacific,' *The Pacific Review*, Vol. 7, No. 4, pp. 367-79.

--(1998) 'The Pacific and Beyond: APEC, ASEM and Regional Economic Management,' in: Grahame Thompson (ed.) *Economic Dynamism in the Asia-Pacific*. London and New York: Routledge, pp. 335-55.

Hrbek, Rudolf and Sabine Weyand (1994) *Betrifft: das Europa der Regionen. Fakten, Probleme Perspektiven*, München: Beck (= Beck'sche Reihe Bd. 1085).

Hund, Markus (1998) *The Making and Development of the Asia-Europe Meeting (ASEM) Context, Strategies and Outcomes*, MA Thesis, University of Freiburg.

Keohane, Robert O. and Joseph S. Nye (1989) *Power and Interdependence. World Politics in Transition*, second edition, Glenview, Ill.: Scott, Foresman.

Lee Chong Wha (1999) Developing an ASEM Position Toward the New WTO Round, Seoul: Korea Institute for International Economic Policy.

Lim, Paul (2000) The Unfolding Asia-Europe Meeting (ASEM) Process: Issues for ASEM III, Paper Presented at the Round Table 'The Future of the ASEM Process,' jointly organized by the European Institute of Asian Studies (Brussels) and the International Institute for Asian Studies (Leiden), Brussels, 3 April 2000.

Maull, Hanns W. (1997) 'Regional Security Cooperation: A Comparison of Europe and East Asia,' *Internationale Politik und Gesellschaft*, No. 1, pp. 49-63.

Maull, Hanns W. and Akihoro Tanaka (1997) 'The Geopolitical Dimension,' in: Council for Asia-Europe Cooperation (ed.) *The Rationale and Common Agenda for Asia-Europe Cooperation*, CAEC Task Force Reports, pp. 31-41.

Mitrany, David (1943) *A Working Peace System. An Argument for the Functional Development of International Organization*. London: The Royal Institute of International Affairs.

Müller, Harald (1993) *Die Chance der Kooperation*. Darmstadt: Wissenschaftliche Buchgesellschaft.

Roloff, Ralf (1998) 'Globalisierung, Regionalisierung und Gleichgewicht,' in: Carlo Masala and Ralf Roloff (Hrsg.), *Herausforderungen der Realpolitik. Beiträge zur Theoriedebatte in der internationalen Politik,* Köln: SH-Verlag, pp. 61-94.

--(1999) 'Europe and Asia: ASEM and Beyond?,' in: Geoffrey Edwards and Elfriede Regelsberger (eds) *Europe's Global Links*, London, second edition (forthcoming).

Rüland, Jürgen (1996) *The Asia-Europe Meeting (ASEM): Towards a New Euro-Asian Relationship?* Universität Rostock: Rostocker Informationen zu Politik und Verwaltung, Heft 5.

--(1998) ASEAN and the Asian Crisis - Repercussions on Regional Cooperation, Paper Prepared for the EUROSEAS 98 Hamburg, Panel 18, Regionalism and Regional Cooperation in Southeast Asia, University of Hamburg, 3-6 September 1998.

--(1999) 'The Future of the ASEM Process: Who, How, Why and What,' in: Wim Stokhof and Paul van der Velde (eds) *ASEM. The Asia-Europe Meeting. A Window of Opportunity*, London and New York: Kegan Paul International, pp. 126-151.

Schirm, Stefan A. (1997) 'Transnationale Globalisierung und regionale Kooperation. Ein Politik-ökonomischer Ansatz zur Erklärung internationaler Zusammenarbeit in Europa und den Amerikas,' *Zeitschrift für internationale Beziehungen*, Vol. 4, No. 1, pp. 69-106.

Schwengel, Hermann (1999) *Globalisierung mit europäischem Gesicht. Der Kampf um die politische Form der Zukunft*. Berlin: Aufbau-Verlag.

Soesastro, Hadi and Simon Nuttall (1997) 'The Institutional Dimension,' in: Council for Asia-Europe Cooperation (ed.) *The Rationale and Common Agenda for Asia-Europe Cooperation*, CAEC Task Force Reports, pp. 75-86.

Synnott, Hilary (1999) 'The Second Asia-Europe Summit and the ASEM Process,' *Asian Affairs*, Vol. XXX, Part I, February, pp. 3-10.

Wyatt-Walter, Andrew (1995) 'Regionalism, Gloablization, and the World Economic Order,' in: Louise Fawcett and Andrew Hurrell (eds) *Regionalism in World Politics. Regional Organization and International Order*. Oxford University Press, pp. 74-120.

Zürn, Michael (1998) *Regieren jenseits des Nationalstaates*. Frankfurt am Main: Suhrkamp, Edition zweite Moderne.

PART THREE

INVENTING AN ASEM VOCABULARY

CHAPTER 7

LEGAL STATUS OF
NON-PROFIT ORGANIZATIONS
IN JAPAN

KIYOKO IKEGAMI

The year 1998 marked the beginning of the new era for private non-profit organizations (NPOs) in Japan. In March 1998, the House of Councillors of the Japanese Diet adopted a draft bill entitled *Act on the Promotion of Specific Non-profit Activities* (NPO Act), which was passed in December 1998. Since its introduction in the Diet in December 1996, the bill had been one of the main issues attracting public concern in Japan as it would enable most of the nations' estimated 86,000 NPO which currently do not have a legal basis for operation to acquire legal status.[1] As lack of legal status had been one of the major institutional obstacles severely limiting the ability of NPOs to perform their social and economic activities, a new legislation to ease the conditions under which the NPOs could acquire legal status had been considered essential to the propitious development of the private non-profit sector in Japan.

The draft bill, which was amended in the House of Councillors, was sent back to the House of Representatives and approved. While it reserved some fundamental issues for future consideration, the bill has been facilitating a revolutionary change in the scale and scope of activity for the Japanese NPOs, especially grassroots non-governmental organizations (NGOs), and is contributing to the further development of civil society in Japan. The social recognition of the role of NGOs in the Hanshin Earthquake as well as the international trend of NGO participation at various levels towards the construction of a civil society have boosted the process.

This article extrapolates an (1) review of the legal system under which the NPOs in Japan were regulated and to problems such bodies had experienced prior to the passing of the bill; (2) an analysis of the process towards new legislature, including the involvement of interested NPOs in recent years; (3) an introduction to the main content of the NPO Act, pointing out the significance of changes the bill has brought about, and (4) a brief review of the progress made during the first year of its implementation, suggesting legal and other measures which will be necessary in the future to promote the role of private non-profit sector in Japan even more.

KIYOKO IKEGAMI

PROBLEMS NPOS FACED PRIOR TO THE NPO ACT

It may be said that, compared to the systems in force in other industrialized countries, the Japanese legal system concerning the status and activities of NPOs is very underdeveloped. The basic law which governs all existing NPOs in the country is the Civil Code, which came into effect soon after the first constitution of Japan was implemented in 1898.

Article 34 of the Civil Code states that an 'incorporated association or foundation relating to worship, religion, charity, science, art or otherwise relating to public interests and not having for its purpose the acquisition of gain, may be made a juristic personality subject to the permission of the competent authorities.' Under this definition of *koeki hojin* (public-interest corporations), a number of organizations which would be counted as NPOs in other countries may not be covered as such. While special laws were created under the Civil Code to cover such categories of organizations as societies, alumni associations, special interest associations, and small-scale volunteer organizations (i.e. those that cannot meet the qualifications for associations or foundations) cannot attain juristic personality because of the absence of such a special law, and must remain organizations without a legal status.[2]

Consequently, although there has been a dramatic increase of so-called NGOs in recent years, most NGOs do not have legal status and are not registered. Most NGOs are inhibited even in pursuing the possibility to acquire incorporated status because there are minimum requirements nowadays of approximately 300 million yen as an endowment and of 30 million yen as an annual budget as well as coming under the auspices of government ministries. Even if they wished to acquire legal status it is usually a process which takes years and the NGOs must run the gauntlet of the bureaucratic red tape of visiting all the relevant ministries. As the ministries are generally reluctant to grant legal status to organizations which voice opposition to the government or its policies, ineluctably the system greatly endangers the independence of NGOs.

Without legal basis for their existence, most NGOs have low social credibility, and it is difficult for them to engage in any significant fundraising and other economic activities. It may be surprising that even internationally known NGOs such as the branch office in Japan of Amnesty International does not have legal status. Its directors have no choice but to make contracts to rent office space, subscribe for telephones, and open bank accounts under their personal responsibility using their own names. The directors are faced with the risk of being personally indebted should the organizations be forced to disband with a budgetary deficit, and the NGOs would be required to pay death duties should the director suddenly die.

The domestic NGOs which operate internationally are also faced with problems because in some recipient countries or international organizations the legal status of the NGOs is an important issue. Lack of human resources is another serious problem for most NGOs, as they are unable to attract well-trained personnel because of their inability to offer good salary or guarantee social security. Because of budgetary constraints, many NGOs are unable even to employ full-time staff. Under these circumstances, the NGOs in Japan have their hands tied and are unable to play their role in society.

The Civil Code has also set the basis for the unique tax exemption system pertaining in Japan for *koeki hojin*, whereby the governing ministry gives permission for incorporation and grants tax exemption without recourse to the independent judgement of the taxation department. As mentioned earlier, this system reinforces government control over private NPOs, because the decision to grant incorporated status and tax exemption status is left to the discretion of the ministry and there is a lack of transparency in the way the standard of approval is decided. Those NPOs which have passed this test are granted a relatively generous corporate tax of 27 per cent on income from profit-making activities, as compared the 37.5 per cent on al income for other companies.

There are also tax incentives for companies and individuals to make donations to NPOs. Donations by companies to some thousand NPOs, which are specially designated by the finance minister as being particularly beneficial to the public (*tokutei koeki zoshin hojin*) can be, deducted at up to twice the normal deduction calculation limits. A similar system is applied to income tax on individuals who make donations to these corporations. It should be noted, however, that these *tokutei koeki zoshin hojin* comprise less than five per cent of all *koeki hojin* and most of them are unequivocally either government-sponsored or created. NPOs without legal status enjoy no tax privileges; they are required to pay 'corporate tax,' although they do not have legal status as corporations, on income from profit-making activities at the same tax rate as private companies.

As the description just given reveals, the NPOs in Japan are seriously constrained in their establishment and operation by the rigid legal system. Those numerous NPOs which do not qualify as *koeki hojin* or which decide not to apply for such status remain without legal status and are tremendously disadvantaged in their social and economic activities. The current situation in which a highly regulated society prevails will continue to inhibit the development of a lively society in which free, autonomous, and diverse activities may be undertaken by citizens' organizations. This is the main background to the NPO Act.

THE PROGRESS TOWARDS THE LEGISLATION OF THE NPO ACT

Before describing the actual legislative process of the NPO Act, it may be necessary to review the recent movements of NGOs in Japan, prior to the NPO Act. A major development in the non-profit sector in Japan in recent years is readily observable in the surge of NGOs active both internationally oriented and domestically oriented in diverse fields. Although initially movements run by citizens in Japan in the post-war period began around two perennial topics, i.e. the consumer movement and the environmental protection movement, they have now broadened their scope to cover a wide variety of themes such as welfare, women, education, global environment, health, culture, international exchange and international co-operation. The nature of these movements has also shifted from the demand-oppose type of movement to the propose-actualize type of movement, perhaps because they have learned from their own experience and from the experience of NGOs abroad that 'commitment' to the decision-making process is more effective in bringing about desired changes than total 'confrontation' with the government.

With this change in attitude public awareness of the important role of NGOs has also increased. The growing attention focused on the activities of NGOs is indicated in a dramatic increase in media coverage of their activities in recent years. According to a keyword search on four major Japanese newspapers, the frequency of articles on NGOs made a jump from 192 during 1991 to 291 in 1992, 972 in 1993, to 1,506 in 1994.[3]

In the 1990s this interest in the non-profit sector has been linked to an active exploration among the Japanese leaders of the respective roles of government and the private sector in the governance of Japanese society, as indicated by the debates raging about critical issues such as 'deregulation' or the need to establish a new social security system in the rapidly ageing society. The enormous fiscal deficit has also been a grudging acknowledgement on the part of some in the government that the NGOs can and are making positive contributions to addressing domestic issues created by a complex, pluralistic society as well as playing their part in the enhancement of external relationships in an increasingly interdependent world. This is the background against which both the NGOs and the policy makers have become aware that in order to expand the scale and scope of NGO activities, it is essential to establish a legal infrastructure which enables the NGOs to pursue their desired goals in the society freely.

In November 1994, about fifty interested NGOs and NGO networks gathered together and established 'NGO Network for the Creation of an Institution which Supports Activities by the Citizens,' with the purpose of drafting new legislation to propose to the decision makers.[4] This was perhaps the first time in the history of the NGO movements in Japan that NGOs with completely different interests were united for a single purpose. The Network, which consisted of major national NGOs and had prominent scholars and lawyers to advise it, was quite successful not only in agreeing on the draft text of the legislation but also in sharing information, negotiating with the policy makers, and raising public awareness during the whole process. Around the same period, some political parties also began to explore the possibility of new legislation on NPOs.

The earthquake in Kobe in January 1995 accelerated this move towards legislation. Immediately after the earthquake, tens of thousands of volunteers from all over the country and also from abroad rushed to the Kobe area to help victims. The paralysis of the government bureaucracy in coping with the situation was contrasted to the great contributions made by NGOs and volunteers. The Japanese public was made aware that the government was not capable of crisis management and the NGOs could be more reliable in some emergency situations in terms of saving people's lives and providing services at grassroots level. In areas such as natural and human-made disasters where the government does not have sufficient flexibility or resources to provide effective responses, the NGOs have pushed into the public realm to claim these areas as their own.

Soon after the earthquake, the legislators in the ruling and opposition parties as well as in the government ministries began working on new legislation on NPOs. One of the first steps was to set up an inter-ministerial working group under the Chief Cabinet Secretary involving eighteen relevant ministries, to work on the legislation in collaboration. Another step was that the three ruling parties (the liberal Democratic Part (LDP), the Social Democratic Party of Japan, and the New Party Sakigake) established a project team to work on their version of the legislation. There was a bitter conflict between the government offices and the legislators in the parliament as to who would prepare and submit legislation to the Diet.

In Japan over eighty per cent of national legislation is prepared for actual drafting and submission to the Diet by the government requiring no more than the approval or amendment by the ruling parties. This time it was different and the ruling parties strongly insisted that the NPO Act be prepared by the legislature, arguing that this consisted of representatives of the citizens whose activities the law is supposed to govern and also that it was impossible for government offices to draw up a law which puts significant limitations on their own power and discretion over the private non-profit sector. As a result, the ruling parties were able to have their way and after two years of intensive discussion among themselves and also involving the NGO network, the ruling parties submitted a draft bill to the House of Representatives entitled 'Act on the Promotion of Citizens

Activities' in December 1996. The bill was debated again and after some revision, the House approved it in June 1997.

The bill was then sent to the House of Councillors for its consideration and approval. But it was not all plain sailing. The LDP members of this House demanded further revisions which included removal of all references to 'citizens' in the title and the text of the bill. While the two other parties in the coalition were sceptical of the intentions of the LDP on this point, they agreed to replace the word 'citizens' with 'non-profit organizations,' except in one place. In the statement on the purpose of the bill, there was a reference to promoting the development of 'citizens' participation in activities which contribute to the benefit of society. Here, the phrase was changed to activities 'carried out by the citizens' to strengthen the position of citizens as an independent actor. Although reduced to only one reference, it is still very significant that the term 'citizen' was retained, as this was the first time it was used in Japanese law. The title of the bill was changed to 'Act on the Promotion of Specific Non-profit Activities,' but, there was little opposition from the NGOs since they had been unable to define 'citizens'' activities.

After this major revision, the House of Councillors and the House of Representatives passed the NPO Act. It must be pointed out that for the NGOs and the policy makers, the legislative process of the NPO Act was as meaningful as the law itself, in terms of creating a new environment in which the two actors may co-operate in a productive manner for the achievement of a common goal. The legislation was a result of a true collaborative effort between the citizens' organizations and the legislature, as the NGOs were actively involved in every stage of the decision-making process. The policy makers were willing to involve NGOs in discussions of the legislation since they believed that a law on citizens' activities could never be effective without the input and commitment of the citizens themselves. It was recognized that the reverse was also true. The two actors constantly exchanged views and negotiated with each other, and there were even instances in which the policy makers had to depend on the advice of the NGOs as they commanded tremendous expertise in the legal system and had first-hand knowledge of the situation of NGOs in Japan.

The legislative process also contributed to strengthening the capacity of the NGOs to organize themselves in order to achieve the realization of their political will. It is worth noting that, while it had been thought impossible for the NGOs with such diverse interests to come to a complete agreement, the various NGOs involved in this legislative process were able to overcome their differences and agree on a single set of proposals, which strengthened their position in negotiating with specific political parties, the three ruling parties, and made a realistic assessment of the political environment, on the basis of which they aimed to achieve a unanimous vote in the Diet, indicates their strong compulsion to accomplish the reforms. The political skills these NGOs have been able to develop are a true sign that citizens can play an even more important role in the political decision making in the future.

THE CONTENT OF THE NPO ACT AND ITS SIGNIFICANCE

Like other special laws concerning some types of non-profit organizations, the NPO Act is established as a special law under Article 34 of the Civil Code. As such, in order to attain a legal status must be considered to be promoting the public interest. The purpose of the law is to grant legal status to non-profit citizens' organizations which engage in activities promoting the benefits of many unspecified persons. The term 'specific non-profit activities' covers health, community development, the environment, and gender equality. Under this system, an activity is automatically conceived of as promoting public interest if it falls under any one of twelve specified areas. The term 'specific' is also intended to exclude those categories of NPOs already covered by other existing special laws such as religious organizations.

Since deciding whether or not an activity is promoting public interest is a subjective question which has been left to the discretion of the competent authority, it is significant that the new law has succeeded in avoiding such subjective considerations by simply assuming that certain areas of activities do promote the public interest. On the other hand, that fact that it singled out twelve areas of activities instead of defining 'specific non-profit activities' may be seen as a legal defect. All is not lost, since the compass of these twelve areas is so broad, there is little concern on the part of the NGOs that some activities may have been omitted from these categories. During the formal Diet meetings, the legislators responsible for drafting the bill guaranteed that all conceivable NGO activities may in some way or another be linked to one of the twelve areas.

The establishment of NPOs is currently based on 'approval (*kyoka*)' by the authority competent to 'endorse (*ninka* or *ninsho*)' their establishment if the organization has met the conditions stipulated in the law. The evaluation by the authority is based solely upon the documents submitted by the organizations, and the decision must be made within three months after receipt of the documents. If the authority decided not to 'endorse' the establishment of an organization, it must notify them of the reasons for non-endorsement in a written form.

This system will certainly pave the way for more NGOs to acquire legal status, since it will greatly limit the discretion by the bureaucracy. 'Endorsement' as conceived in the NPO Act goes far beyond the general concept of the term to resemble the 'registration' of private companies in some respects, since there is little room for the authority to make substantial judgement. This can be seen as a clear example of the deregulation of the non-profit sector in Japan. Some NGOs argued in the legislative process that there is no need for 'approval,' 'endorsement' or any type of government evaluation in the establishment of NGOs, and that the NPOs should be automatically considered corporate entities if they meet the legal require-ments as organizations and make the establishment public by following certain procedures. Such is the case with private companies in Japan.

While it is currently the relevant ministries in the central government which approve the establishment of NPOs and oversee their activities, under the new system, the onus of 'competent authority' would be shifted to the governor of the prefecture in which the office of the organization is located. The exception to this provision would be organizations with offices in more than one prefecture, in which case the Director-General of the National Economic Planning Agency should be the competent authority. This shift in the designation of the competent authority is a significant move towards decentralization, as each prefectural governor will be able to act on his own behalf instead of merely implementing national policies at the local level. Under the NPO Act, the prefectures are empowered to implement their own statutes and regulations. That fact that this may result in different treatment of NPOs in different prefectures should not be seen as a problem, since the prefectures would be able to make policies to suit the various local characteristics and needs. The law also provides for limitation of discretion and safeguards against abuse of NPOs. It is stated, for instance, that the competent authority cannot invalidate its 'endorsement' for an organization unless there has been a clear violation of the law by the organization. It should also be noted that the designation of a single organ as the competent authority, i.e. prefectural governor or the National Economic Planning Agency, will solve the problems associated with bureaucratic division and therefore, facilitate a more efficient response by the authority.

Another important aspect of the NPO Act is the obligation of the NPOs to disclose their annual report and other information relating to the administration and budgetary situation of the organization to the general public. Under their previous legal status, the NPOs were required to submit this information to the competent authority but they had no obligation towards the general public. By adding this obligation, the new law is designed to expose the performance of the NPOs to citizens and enhance the transparency of their activities. It may also be said that this also makes it easier for NPOs to manage their own performance. In the future the social and economic position of the NPOs will not be based on their legal and fiscal status but will depend more upon how the public evaluates their performance.

THE REVIEW OF ONE YEAR ACHIEVEMENT
AND THE FUTURE AGENDA

The Tokyo Metropolitan government, for example, approved twelve NPO applications out of 138 as of 31 May and 220 NPOs as of 30 November 1999.[5] One thousand and five NPOs out of 1,524 applications obtained legal status in Japan in the one year since the implementation of the NPO Act. The majority of these NPOs engage in welfare activities at the community level. However, the number of applications itself was much less than had been expected. The reason for this dearth of applications has been analysed as hesitation to apply on the part of the NPOs.[6] They cannot decide whether they should apply for legal status or not, weighing up the pros and cons between obligations like submitting an annual report and a financial report, and merits derived from legal status. Pertinently the tax exemption status was not granted in the NPO Act, and this is considered to be the most effective means for NPOs to keep their heads above water.

The 'Yui no Kai' can be said to be a typical NPO which was granted legal status after the implementation of the NPO Act. It has been an NPO with eight years experience in Nagoya Prefecture where it is active in assisting the aged. It discussed the application to acquire the legal status with its members for more than a year. They made an application based on their consensus in April 1999 and were granted legal status in August 1999. The members are aware of the role of civic organizations in the restructuring of the community and the society at large. Their vision is clear and they believe that citizens have to contribute to tackle social issues in ways which may be different from those adopted by the local government and private sectors, but may need co-ordination and collaboration. In terms of their mission, they regard the ageing society as a social problem, but at the same time they aim at establishing a society in which everyone can enjoy longevity through the participation of their fellow citizens.[7]

Although reform of the tax laws was considered during the legislative process of the NPO Act, allowing the granting of tax privileges to NPOs covered by the bill, the issue was left open for future discussions as reforming all relevant tax laws might take a considerable amount of time. The revision of the Civil Code to establish a comprehensive law which covers all types of NPOs is an even more difficult task requiring a review of all the special laws existing under the Code. While these two issues were not mentioned in the actual text of the NPO Act, they were included in the

Attached Resolution which was adopted by a unanimous vote in the Diet. In the Resolution it is stated that the government must launch considerations of these two issues (tax exemption and the revision of the Civil Code) and reach a conclusion within two years from the date of the implementation of the NPO Act.

After one year of citizens' activities to advocate the promotion of tax exemption status for NPOs, the Parliamentarians Federation to Promote and Support NPOs as well as a Special Committee on NPOs of the LDP formulated their proposals to change the present tax system for December 1. However, the Ministry of Finance showed its resistance to the proposed changes.[8] The review and the process of negotiation through discussion are still expected to be continued in the Diet for another year but citizens will also be involved.

One of the hindrances standing in the way of a growth in scale of Japanese NPOs is argued to be the refusal to grant them tax exemption status. One indication of this is shown by the different levels of funds raised by NGOs engaging in international co-operation, one of twelve areas specified in the NPO Act. Japanese NGOs could only raise one-fifteenth of the sum raised by their US equivalents.[9] Individuals and private corporations could support NGOs much more if tax exemption was granted in Japan.

There is an urgent need on the part of the non-profit sector in Japan to promote institution building and human resource development. Independent and innovative activities undertaken by NPOs cannot be ensured of success unless these organizations have a strong institutional and staff capacity. As has been discussed above, the budgetary constraints arising from the lack of tax privileges may be a negative factor affecting this requirement considerably. Hope is in sight as the institutional constraints are now in the process of reform and there will soon be little justification for not improving the competence and professional expertise of NPOs.

After the NPO Act was passed some prefectural governments established training courses on finance reporting and the tax system as a part of the capacity building of NPO staff. This helps NPOs to comply with their reporting obligation, which leads to the transparency in the activities of the NPOs in promoting their accountability to society. The Charity Commission of the UK could be a model as the third party which could act as a watchdog on the activities of charitable organizations for the public interest.

Any future growth of NPOs in Japan will require vision, funds, and the staff to carry out their activities which are consequently geared to gaining the trust of the society by making themselves accountable to that society. At the same time, the supporting system for legal status, tax exemption, review and checking devices of their activities by third party has to be identified, discussed, and established.

Can NPOs offer Japanese society an alternative channel of quality offering services and information, reallocation of wealth, promotion of decentralization of authority, and the creation of employment? The development of a civil society in Japan depends upon the determined efforts of the non-profit sector.

NOTES

1. This estimate is taken from the speech by Senator Kumashiro in Proceedings of the House of Representatives Cabinet Committee, May 28, 1997.
2. Tadashi Yamamoto. The Non-profit Sector in Japan, in: The Johns Hopkins Comparative Non-profit Sector Project 1994, p. 4.
3. Ibid., p. 1.
4. To contact the NGO Network for the Creation of an Institution which Support Activities by Citizens: matubara@vcom.or.jp
5. *Yomiuri Newspaper*, June 1, 1999. Nihon Keizai Newspaper, November 30, 1999.
6. *Mainichi Newspaper*, December 1, 1999.
7. Presentation by Ms Noriko Matsushita, president of Yui no Kai on September 16, 1999 at the Royal Institute of International Affairs, London.
8. *Asashi Newspaper*, November 30, 1999.
9. Ministry of Foreign Affairs, Japanese ODA Report, 1995, p. 282.

CHAPTER 8

METHODS FOR FACILITATING INTEGRATION OF DEVELOPING NATIONS INTO THE ASEM PROCESS

NGYUEN SON

The trade relationship between the two continents of Asia and Europe is an undisputed factor of human history. Two thousand years ago or more, the famous Silk Road spanned the mountains and deserts of the centre of the Asian continent to link some of the most ancient civilizations on earth. These commercial ties were maintained during the most prosperous eras of the feudal dynasties in Asia. Throughout the centuries, the commercial relationship between Europe and Asia has fluctuated in response to historical changes. The forms that it has taken have also varied according to international circumstances as well as to the political and developmental level of the countries on both continents.

Though poised at different stages of development, these countries are now facing great challenges, most of which will require the joint efforts of nations to solve and which will need solutions to be found at a global level. These dilemmas include the attainment of stable economic growth, tackling unemployment, sorting out immigration, and the hazards facing the environment. It was under these circumstances that the ASEM was launched, carrying the hope of its twenty-five members that it would gather momentum in promoting co-operation and development by exploiting the potential of the two continents. Following in the wake of more than two millennia of historical changes, the ASEM process should be cherished as the first milestone on the Silk Road for the twenty-first century.

EFFORTS TOWARDS INTEGRATION MADE BY ASIAN DEVELOPING COUNTRIES

The process of forming an economic alliance leading to trade and investment promotion has been considered to be a remedy for economic recovery and as a dynamic source of development by most developing members of ASEM. The Association of Southeast Asian Nations (ASEAN), involving ten countries from within the region, is taking measures to push the formation of the ASEAN Free Trade Area (AFTA) by the year 2006.

While this process is under way, the East Asia Economic Co-operation based on ASEAN+3 (Japan, Korea, and China) is being strengthened. A joint statement on East Asian co-operation approved by the leaders of these countries in 1999 has defined the guiding rules for co-operation in the fields of finance, science and technology, culture and education.

Simultaneously, domestic reforms designed to lead towards a market economy aided and abetted by trade and investment promotion are being pursued by each nation so as to create a favourable climate in which business may flourish. Learning bitter lessons from the Asian financial monetary crisis, these newly industrialized countries as well as those with economies in transition are pushing their market-oriented economic reforms, purifying their management apparatuses and adjusting legal systems to bring these into conformity with international rules. Take China as an example. In its negotiations for accession to the WTO, this country has made a considerable effort to open what are said to be sensitive markets such as telecommunications, banking and insurance to foreign investment. Conscious of the urgent need to improve the environment for foreign investment to cope with growing competition among regions in the context of globalization, while they are carrying out domestic reforms, the ASEAN countries are also negotiating measures to implement the ASEAN Investment Area and staging campaigns to boost investment into the region. Following the initiative taken by the prime minister of Singapore, Goh Chok Tong in March this year, a joint ASEAN mission to Japan was undertaken to update investors on the current economic situation and investment opportunities in the region. A few more missions are planned to various destinations in the US and Europe.

An improvement of the integration capacity of the developing countries will indubitably contribute to the success of globalization and to the ASEM process in particular. The major obstacles to the integration of the countries into the international business environment stems from the objective factor of their low level of development. The major current problems facing most of the ASEM developing members can be listed as follows: rudimentary systems of law bristling with a large number of incompatibilities to international rules, underdeveloped infrastructures, plus limited financial and human resources. These impede the developing countries from taking any bold steps and participating actively and zealously in the process of integration. The implementation of the WTO Customs Valuation Agreement is an example. Developing countries will suffer not only from the decrease in revenue from import-export taxes, but they will also feel the lack of a material technical base from which to supervise imports and exports as well as being able to limit commercial fraud when transferring from an import-export taxation system based on a minimum price list to one based on contracted prices. The upshot is that taxation on the basis of a minimum price list still exists despite its contradiction to WTO rules. Therefore, being fully aware of the potential advantages of globalization, these governments are still wavering between the benefits they would gain and the possible subsequent threat to economic stability, national sovereignty, and cultural values. At the dawn of the twenty-first century, they should find the answer to the question of whether they are able to manage the integration process and whether, conversely, its adverse side effects may interfere with their socio-economic development.

Meanwhile, a stable and sustainable trade system has to ensure that the active and zealous participation of its members and harmonize the immediate and long-term interests between groups of nations. The failure of the WTO ministerial meeting in Seattle to launch the Millennium Round of trade negotiations and the dissident voices raised at the UNCTAD-X forum show that present-day international trade is not a field dominated by some of the richest countries. Integrating itself into the world trade system, each nation has the right to benefit from the growth in world-wide trade and at the same time has assumed the obligation to carry out market-opening commitments which take into consideration the inequality in level of development. The modern terms of international trade development do not simply mean an increase in absolute volume of trade. Trade-development thinking should move beyond pure trade growth to encompass such important goals as the enhanced participation of all nations in international trade, the reduction of the disproportion between rich and poor nations, and an improved quality of life for all.

The ASEM's objective in motivating equal co-operation for the mutual benefit of all and eliminating aid-based trade relations is in line with the basic rules of world trade and the general development trend. Progress towards these goals requires appropriate forms of co-operation oriented towards improving the integration capacity of developing members so as to bridge the disparity in the level of development between the two groups of nations. The improved capacity will greatly assist these governments in steering their trade and investment protection policies in the direction of openness and more intensive participation in market access negotiations. Therefore, ASEM equal partnership should be understood as co-operation based on mutual benefits with preferential policies from developed countries to support resource-development programmes in the developing countries.

ENHANCED SCIENTIFIC AND TECHNOLOGICAL CO-OPERATION AND INVESTMENT PROMOTION

In order to achieve this objective, the co-operation between the two continents within the ASEM framework in the fields of science – technology and investment promotion should be given high priority. The foremost reason for doing so it that these are areas in which the two continents possess great potential and can supplement each other. A second compelling reason is the fact that co-operation in these fields may contribute directly to raising the capacity of developing countries effectively.

The science and technological expertise, which provided the basis for the predominance of Europe over the world in the past, is inexorably affirming its role as a fundamental basis and instrument for development at present as well as in the future. Besides the advantages in knowledge and working experience, ASEM developed countries are also financially capable of allocating budgets for research and development activities. In contrast, the funding for such activities in the ASEM developing countries has remained very modest, despite certain efforts on the part of their governments. Some ASEM developing countries have a considerable number of engineers and scientists who have been systematically trained and are well qualified. However, hampered by limited funding and the lack of modern laboratory equipment and poor research facilities in general, these scientists cannot work to their full capacity and so make new steps forward.

This being the case, appropriate co-operation programmes at national level or between research institutes in ASEM member countries will benefit all partners. Developed countries can carry out their research utilizing the grey matter from the developing countries. This is not simply poaching on the preserves of others because the latter will also pick the fruits of such co-operation. On the one hand, they will be able to absorb the results of new research and, on the other, it is very meaningful for scientists to be able to exploit their own knowledge, improve their qualifications, and broaden their work experience, and all the while learn the latest and most advanced methods of performing research work. Recently, through an exchange programme for researchers and education assistance, a number of students and scientists have been trained or have improved their qualifications in countries with advanced science and technology. After returning home, they make a valuable contribution to human resources development and the enhancement of the research capacities of their home countries. Within the ASEM framework, the first Meeting of Science and Technology Ministers, held in Beijing in October last year, adopted eleven science and technology co-operation programmes between member countries. However, this is just the beginning of the process, which requires further detailed deployment in a way which will enable the mobilization of resources from ASEM members and assure the effectiveness of the projects.

Foreign Direct Investment (FDI) has long played an important role in economic growth and development: foreign capital played a critical role in the early states of development of many of today's industrialized economies, including the US, Canada, and Australia. As the processes of globalization have accelerated in the last fifteen years, foreign investment, and particularly foreign direct investment, has become a key ingredient in the growth and competitiveness of developed and developing economies alike. FDI is a major vehicle for developing economies to catch up with more advanced countries as it provides access to foreign savings, technology, management skills, and access to export markets. In this fashion, FDI makes a significant contribution to improving the capacity for the rapid integration of developing countries into the world economy. As FDI focuses mainly on manufacturing and service industries, the structural adjustment process in these countries will be steered in the direction of a greater proportion of industries and services in the economy. Through investment projects for infrastructure, facilities for international integration will be strengthened, especially the telecommunications and transport systems. The financial and banking sectors, which are usually cited as disadvantages of the ASEM developing members, could be efficiently reorganized and rehabilitated thanks to the presence of foreign financial groups.

The EU represents the world's largest economic region. With the introduction of the Euro, the EU has now also become an enormous capital market. Although the investment flow from European members to Asian members within the ASEM framework has grown rapidly over the last decade, the European share is lower than that of the principal sources of investment in Asia, namely the United States, and intra-regional Asian investment including Japanese direct investment. The under-representation is a reflection of the fact that EU investors have traditionally focused on investment opportunities within their own region and when looking further afield tend to look at Central and Eastern Europe. Nevertheless, predictions about the economic development of the Asia-Pacific region in the next decade show that this region offers promising potential for large, long-term investment. Therefore, in addition to the effort made by these ASEM members to improve their investment environment, it is essential that the EU should take measures to encourage investment flows to these countries, a move which would step up their rehabilitation and accelerate their subsequent painless integration into the world economy, creating favourable conditions for their active and diversified participation in ASEM co-operative activities.

So far, in the four years of its existence, ASEM has booked certain achievements. To accelerate the ASEM process towards the goals set out by the Vision Group, including a Asia-Europe free trade area by the year 2025, it is essential to set in motion a co-operation strategy which is able to harmonize the interest of parties and improve the capacity of developing members. Hopefully, leaders of ASEM countries will lay down the long-term strategy to take the ASEM process forward into the twenty-first century for the development and waxing prosperity of all our nations.

REFERENCES

United Nations Conference on Trade and Development (UNCTAD), *World Investment Report 1998*, Unites Nations, Vienna, 1998.

Commission of the EU, *Commissions Recommendations for the Broad Guideline of the Economic Policies of the Member States and the Community*, Brussel, 1999.

The World Bank, *World Development Report 1999/2000*, New York, 1999.

CHAPTER 9

EUROPE'S ROLE IN ASIAN SECURITY

DALJIT SINGH

It can be said without exaggeration that at the dawn of the new millennium, Western Europe no longer had a serious security threat, at any rate not a conventional one. This must be something quite new in the continent's troubled history. Admittedly there are still problems in the Balkans, but these are being managed and will probably be resolved within this decade. Russia remains a source of uncertainty but is likely to be preoccupied with domestic affairs for the rest of the decade.

In looking for the causes of this happy state of affairs, two factors must surely stand out. One is the North Atlantic Treaty Organisation (NATO), with the US at its core, and the other the phenomenon of European integration. NATO and American power maintained peace and stability in Europe in the face of nearly a half century of Soviet threat. European integration healed the historical divisions and suspicions between European countries.

A peaceful, prosperous, democratic Europe is a boon to the world, and not just economically. It will no longer be the source of global wars. It is a measure of the transformation of Europe that this is now taken for granted, considering the fact that the two cataclysmic world wars of the twentieth century were of European origin.

Wars with major global economic and security consequences take place only between great powers. If Europe and North America are zones of peace, that leaves Asia as the third region of great and potentially great powers. Unfortunately, compared with North America and the European Union, Asia has some way to go to become a region of durable peace, stability and prosperity. Asia is trying hard to move in this direction, but there are still many pitfalls. The developed part of Asia is small, only Japan really, together perhaps with tiny Singapore and Hong Kong. South Korea and Taiwan are in the next tier, followed by the rapidly developing parts of Asia - the coastal provinces of China, some ASEAN countries, and parts of India.

The central argument of this paper is that it is in the enlightened self-interest of the two regions that have 'arrived', i.e. achieved peaceful, prosperous and stable societies to help the third great region of economic dynamism, namely Asia, to manage its transitions. The US is already deeply engaged strategically and politically in Asia, especially East Asia, but Europe is not. It only wants to sell airbuses and cars to Asia.

WHY EUROPE NEEDS TO BE ENGAGED

There are good reasons why Europe should, in its own interest, take a renewed political and security interest in Asia to help construct a stable system of international relations. Firstly, Europe has vital economic interests in East Asia. Notwithstanding the recent economic crisis, the shift of economic power to East Asia has been phenomenal. In 1960 the share of East Asia of world GNP was 4 per cent. In 1995 it was about 25 per cent. The Asian economic crisis exposed weaknesses in state and corporate governance. But in 1999 Asia was again the world's fastest growing region. As the Asian Development Bank states: 'The transformation of developing Asia from financial crisis in 1997-98 to the world's fastest growing region has exceeded all expectations. It took developing Asia less than two years to return to pre-crisis level of industrial production.'[1] There is little doubt that as the twenty-first century progresses, the growth of the economic power of East Asia will continue, though the pace may be slower than once envisaged. This is because major regions with large populations, like China (1.2 billion) and Southeast Asia (500 million), are only in the early stages of industrialization.

Europe knows that it has no choice but to engage in deep economic interaction with East Asia. Cutting itself off from such a dynamic economic region would be tantamount to inviting its own economic decline. Hence it is no surprise that in 1996, the European Union's two-way trade with East Asia, at US$302 billion, was larger than the EU's two-way trade with the US (US$295.4 billion). EU banks lent much more to Asia (US$106 billion) than American banks (US$18 billion) and Japanese banks (US$68 billion).[2] EU countries also have substantial foreign direct investment (FDI) in East Asia. According to EUROSTAT the stock of EU FDI in eight of the ASEM countries (the original five ASEAN countries plus China, Japan, and South Korea) was about 36 billion in European Currency Units in 1995.

Secondly, East Asia is also the region where the interests of four major powers, US, China, Japan, and Russia, intersect. Because of its global economic importance and the involvement of the interests of these great powers, peace or war in Asia would have global repercussions.

The policies and postures of two of these powers, the US and Russia, are of great importance to Europe and they could in the future be significantly affected by developments in Asia. The US is both an Atlantic and a Pacific power, with growing interests in East Asia where it still maintains 100,000 forward deployed troops and has bilateral security treaties with five states in the Western Pacific - Japan, South Korea, Philippines, Thailand, and Australia. The US is also the key military ally of Europe in NATO. In so far as the global policies and the deployment of the political and military resources of the US are affected by Asian developments - and this could be increasingly so in the future - they could have a significant bearing on European affairs.

For the next decade this will apply less to Russia, which is both a European and Asian power, because it is likely to be weak and preoccupied with domestic affairs. But when it regains its poise and strength it too is likely to be more engaged with the strong Asian powers on its doorstep. Indeed, over the longer term, Asian affairs could have significant effects on the posture Russia adopts in Europe, as they did in the early part of the twentieth century.

Thirdly, Asia contains the world's most populous countries. Conflict in Asia and failures in development there could result in tidal waves of illegal immigrants to the richer developed world, including Europe. Economic growth will also lead to stronger military capabilities - already Asia is the fastest growing market for armaments producers.

SECURITY CHALLENGES IN ASIA

East Asia today is at peace, but it is an insecure peace, hedged by uncertainty about the future. The Korean peninsula, the Taiwan Straits and the South China Sea remain potential flash points. There are also many territorial and border disputes. In South Asia there is danger of conflict between nuclear powers India and Pakistan, which, if it occurs, would not be without repercussions on East Asia, given the geopolitical linkages between the two regions. All this does not mean that conflict in East Asia is inevitable. Indeed, as is discussed below, much is already being done to build trust and confidence and to try to work towards an East Asian community and an Asia-Pacific community. Yet it would be wishful thinking to believe that the dangers do not exist.

A central security challenge in East Asia in the first half of the twenty-first century would be the peaceful management of the rise of new powers, principally China and to a lesser extent a more 'normal' Japan, so that both these powers can take their rightful place as peaceful and prosperous great powers on the Asian and world stages.[3] Asia, America, and Europe do not want a repetition of the failures, with horrendous consequences, in managing the rise of new powers, imperial Germany in Europe and Japan in Asia, in the first half of the twentieth century.

Moreover this transition will be taking place during a period of profound change in the economies and societies within East Asian countries, which does not make for a stable and predictable environment. East Asian countries are undergoing a historic transformation from rural-based economies and societies to modern industrial and service economies. In Europe such a transformation spread over two centuries led to revolutions, civil wars and wars between states. Asia certainly wants to avoid the pre-World War II past of Europe. However, change in Asia has been even faster, and is now being spurred by the new forces of globalization. With such rapid change, old structures, institutions, and relationships are subjected to tremendous stress.

Instability within countries could lead to deterioration in interstate relations through spillover effects or because regimes seek to stay on in power by resorting to nationalism and harnessing it to external causes.

ASIA'S RESPONSE

Asia has taken steps to cope with the challenge posed to the existing system of international relations in Asia by the rise of new powers. First, it has been trying to ensure that there is no destabilizing power vacuum while the changes in power relativities are taking place. Since 1945 American power in the region has maintained the peace behind which economic development could take place. Its continuation, together with the US-Japan security alliance, is essential to the stability in strategic relations in the region, a stability behind which China and Southeast Asia can modernize and Japan can decide how to proceed towards being a more normal country. A US withdrawal will unleash destabilising rivalries between the major Asian powers. Secondly, Asia is trying to promote peace and stability through institution building and co-operative security. In Southeast Asia there is ASEAN which has done quite a good job in confidence building and minimizing the chances of interstate conflict in the geographical area covered by the Association, notwithstanding the challenges it has been facing over the past few years. In the broader Asia-Pacific region, until recently, there was a conspicuous lack of common institutions. However, over the past twelve years, two major Asia-Pacific wide institutions at the official level have been established.

The Asia Pacific Economic Co-operation (APEC) forum was set up in 1989 and seeks to promote trade liberalization and economic co-operation. Its annual informal leaders' meeting is of broader political significance as it allows the heads of government of Asia-Pacific countries to come together in an informal summit and to have bilateral meetings on the side. The other institution, the ASEAN Regional Forum (ARF) is a co-operative security endeavour set up in 1994. It discusses security issues and has undertaken various confidence-building measures. The EU is a member of the ARF.

More recently, East Asia has taken the first steps towards what it hopes will one day result in the establishment of an East Asian free trade area and community. ASEAN Secretary-General, Rudolf C. Severino, described the third summit meeting of East Asian leaders (the ASEAN Plus Three, i.e. the 10 ASEAN countries plus China, Japan and South Korea) after the informal ASEAN summit in Manila in November 1999 as 'part of a general convergence of purpose in Asia, a process that has been building up'. He went on to say: '... the developing forum may serve to diffuse any potential rivalries among the stronger countries of East Asia ... could give the region a stronger voice in international financial decisions ...'[4] There have been meetings of finance ministers and heads of central banks of the thirteen countries. Foreign ministers and trade ministers will also meet while summit meetings of the thirteen countries are expected to continue on an annual basis after the annual ASEAN informal and formal summits.

THE EUROPEAN ROLE

How can Europe assist or co-operate with Asia in relation to the security challenges facing Asia? First, Europe can make a valuable contribution to the co-operative security endeavours of Asia. It has experience and expertise in areas like military confidence-building, in preventive diplomacy and peacekeeping. It can impart this expertise through Track One and Track Two forums connected with the ARF, and it has in fact already been doing so. It may not be possible to implant all the European approaches and techniques in East Asian soil because of East Asia's different histories and political cultures, but this constraint should not be an obstacle to learning from the European experience, and adapting from it for Asian conditions where this is possible.

Second, Asia can also learn from Europe in institution building, notwith-standing the fact that ASEAN has taken pride in its informal approach to problems. The building of a European community itself, from the modest beginnings to the European Union, and its expansion to new members, has been a remarkable achievement. Asia can learn from the European experience on matters like the obligations of existing members of the EU, the criteria for admission of new ones, the origin and evolution of the many political, economic and other institutions which bind the EU countries together, and the work of the Conference for Security and Co-operation in

Europe (CSCE) work and of its successor the Organisation for Security and Co-operation in Europe (OSCE) work. Asia could also look at the European experience on how regionalism can be made more broadly based rather than being confined largely to governmental and quasi-governmental elites.

But, most importantly, Europe should be concerned with the big issues in East Asia which have been touched upon earlier because of their importance to global power relations and security, in particular the future roles of China and Japan, the US-China relationship and the US posture in Asia. Europe has left a rich legacy of ideas and culture in Asia through centuries of past association, much of it still valued and admired. Ideas of Christianity, freedom and democracy, and socialism came to East Asia from Europe, as did the English and French languages, Shakespeare, and Beethoven. This legacy, together with the fact that Europe has no interest in dominating any part of Asia, should make it easier for Europe to use its influence for benign strategic and security ends.

JAPAN AND THE US-JAPAN ALLIANCE

While the US-Japan security relationship is crucial to Asian stability, it is unrealistic to expect Japan, in the changing situation in Asia, to remain a mere 'aircraft carrier' for the US. Japan increasingly feels that it has an international obligation to do more for the stability and security of East Asia. New realities will be propelling Japan in this direction. They include the rise of China, the potential for instability or conflict on the Korean peninsula together with the possession of WMDs by North Korea, and because the US itself is likely to nudge Japan in this direction in the interest of burden sharing. Finally, the new Guidelines approved by the Diet in 1999 for Japanese logistical support to American forces in the event the latter are involved in conflict in the vicinity of Japan are likely to put Japanese personnel in harm's way and affect its relations with neighbouring powers. This prospect itself could lead Japan to seek more military capability so as to have a stronger voice in Washington on security issues of concern.

And the case for Japan to exercise a larger political and security role in Asian affairs, in alliance with the US, may gradually be becoming more persuasive to many in Asia, despite the lingering memories of World War II. After all, Japan has contributed enormously to East Asian economic stability and development. For instance, recently it has given out some US$70 billion out of a promised US$80 billion to countries affected by the Asian economic crisis, including its contributions to IMF packages to three countries.[5] Its international behaviour over the past half a century has been responsible.

99

However, the passage of Japan to a more normal statehood in which it exercises a bigger role in Asian affairs would require a delicate transition domestically and regionally. It is to be hoped that democracy in Japan will remain robust through these changes and that there will never be any doubt that a more respectful place for the military will be within the parameters of civilian control. Regionally, a more normal Japan could arouse anxieties in some countries. However, multilateral mechanisms to engage Japan and to anchor it firmly in a peaceful regional community are already in existence: APEC, the ARF, and the budding East Asian regionalism through the ASEAN Plus Three process.

Europe should be mindful of the importance of this transition to Asian and global security and do whatever it can, through diplomacy and intellectual exchanges, to assist. There is much that Japan has admired in European science and culture and it has enjoyed close relations with European powers at various times since the Meji Restoration, including an alliance with Britain in the early years of the twentieth century. Among present European leaders, President Chirac has a special affection for Japanese culture and has visited Japan many times. Europe can engage Japan in the G-8 process, in the UN and bilaterally, in addition to the ARF and ASEM processes, in dialogues which are not just economic, but involve political and security issues. European scholars and thinkers, in conjunction with their Japanese and American counterparts, should consider ways and means through which Japan could play a larger role in Asian and world affairs, so that it wins the respect and recognition it deserves, without having to strike out as an independent military power. In this context institutions like the IMF and the World Bank, created in a very different world environment, cannot be maintained as the exclusive preserves of America and Europe when Japan is the world's second largest economy and East Asia accounts for 25 per cent of the global economy. Cogently Japan's desire to be a permanent member of the UN Security Council deserves serious consideration.

Japan and the US-Japan alliance are just too important to world peace to be left just to the Americans and the Japanese because of periodic bitter acrimonious in US-Japan relations over economic issues which can sour public goodwill towards the alliance, the tendency of the Americans to be overbearing, and the tendency of the Japanese to be parochial.[6]

CHINA

Even more importantly, Europe should contribute to facilitating the rise of China as a peaceful great power and a responsible member of the Asian family and the world community of nations. Apart from Weapons of Mass Destruction, there is perhaps no other issue of greater importance to Asian and global peace and stability during the first half of the new century. Given its size, rapidly growing economy, not to mention its central geographic location in East Asia, China is set to play a major role in Asian affairs. It is also a permanent member of the UN Security Council.

The rise of China as a great power in the community of nations will be complicated by processes of domestic change. When a country of 1.2 billion people undergoes change from a rural to an industrial and urban society over several decades, disruptions and dislocations are almost inevitable. Economic transformation also places great stress on the political super-structure, as any good Marxist would know. The resulting regime insecurity could lead to a resort to nationalism to rally public support. The historical baggage of bullying and humiliation by the West also provides potential for exploitation for nationalistic purposes.

The easing of China into the modern, rule-based system of international relations is an enormously complex and important challenge. China is an old and great civilization but as a modern nation state it is young. Despite the remarkable economic progress of the last two decades it is still lacking in many institutions of a modern state, like proper legal and banking systems and accountability. Pertinently, its international reflexes are not always in accord with the modern system of international relations.

How America handles China is of course of critical importance, and how China relates to America is perhaps more important than how it relates to any other country. However China and America have too many hang-ups about each other. Japan cannot do much to help because of the historical baggage of Sino-Japanese relations. Europeans are geographically distant and can probably take a more detached and rational approach towards China than either the US or Japan; they should be active in making inputs on China in America, in Japan, and with the Chinese themselves.

However in dealing with China, Europeans need to have a long-term strategic perspective. China policy cannot be dictated just by commercial expediency as seems to be the case today. Nor can it be shaped solely by the pressures of domestic human rights groups in Europe. It has to have a carefully considered mix of elements with the long-term objective of allowing China more space and importance in Asian and world affairs in a rule based system. What China becomes will be shaped in important ways by how the outside world, particularly the major powers, relate to it.

Hard Security

Britain still has military ties with Southeast Asia through its membership of the Five Power Defence Arrangements, together with Malaysia, Singapore, Australia, and New Zealand. They are valuable and should be maintained. Britain also has a residual bilateral security association with Brunei. There are also bilateral links between other countries in Europe and countries of East Asia. For instance, over the past few years, a number of links have been established between France and Singapore, including the stationing in France of a detachment of fighter aircraft from the Republic of Singapore Air Force for training purposes and the deployment of a squadron of French Mirage 2000s to Singapore for up to a week once every two years. On the whole, it would be desirable for Europeans to expand military links with East Asia and Australasia in areas like naval visits, exercises, and training.

However, the burdens of hard security in Asia have to be borne principally by Asians and Americans. It is difficult to envisage Europe playing a major role. Unlike the US, Europe is not a great military power with a global reach, though the European family of nations has a number of former great powers. The civil wars in the former Yugoslavia, starting with Bosnia, showed that Europe on its own could not play an effective role - diplomatic and military - to make a significant difference even in its own backyard. It was the Americans who made the difference.

Perhaps the most significant contribution the Europeans can make in hard security is to develop their own military capabilities to take on larger responsibilities for security on the European continent and in adjacent areas outside Europe, through a European component of NATO. This will leave the US with more resources to contribute to the management of the international system in Asia. It is not right that Europe, which is more dependent on Persian Gulf oil than the US, leaves it mostly to the Americans to shoulder the burdens of Gulf region security. After all, the GDP of the European Union is larger than that of the US while that of NATO Europe is about three-quarters of that of the US. In 1998 the defence expenditure of NATO Europe was 2.1 per cent of GDP compared to 3.2 per cent for the US. For the same year per capita defence expenditure in US dollars was US$396 for NATO Europe compared with US$982 for the US.[7]

Conclusion

Perhaps because of its exertions during nearly half a century of Cold War and the advent of peace without major security threats in the 1990s, Europe seems set to continue with its posture of indulgent self-preoccupation seen over the past decade. When life is so comfortable and peaceful, it is easy to leave the burdens of maintaining peace in more distant regions to others.

However, economic and geopolitical developments in East Asia in the new century will have global repercussions. If the West wants to shape world affairs in the direction of civil, rule-based behaviour, then both the US and Europe have to be seized with the Asian drama and actively engaged to help steer change in a benign direction. European engagement of the nature outlined in this essay will add a third dimension to existing dialogue and co-operative efforts within East Asia through the ASEAN Plus Three mechanism and within the Asia-Pacific through the ARF and APEC. It will bring European experience and expertise to bear upon East Asian problems.

But to play such a role, Europe must be convinced that it has a stake in Asian security and that it is prepared to invest money and effort for deeper engagement. This will require, among other things, the development of more expertise on the politics, security, cultures and languages of at least the more pivotal countries in East Asia like China, Japan, Indonesia, Korea, Vietnam, and Thailand in universities and think tanks in Europe. The best and brightest of European diplomats should be posted not just to Washington, Moscow, or the major European capitals but also to countries of Asia. Only such changes will reflect a genuinely stronger interest by Europe in the politics and security of Asia.

America and Europe together worked hard for half a century to banish the scourge of major war from Europe. Asians and Americans will be working hard to do the same in Asia. America is a young nation, with a short history, compared with the leading European countries. It can be prone to ideological fervour and unilateralism. The constancy of its policies can also be affected by shifting constellations of interest groups and vagaries of public opinion - such is the nature of American democracy. The Europeans have a longer history of statecraft and diplomacy. Equipped with the necessary expertise on Asia, Europe can be a wise and steadying counsel to the US, just as it was in dealing with the Soviet Union during the forty-five years of Cold War confrontation between the two blocs in Europe. It will be a valuable addition to the counsel the US receives from Asia itself, the value of which can be limited by suspicion, as in the case of China, or the culture of politeness, as in the case of Japan. Moreover, it will carry weight in the corridors of power in Washington.

NOTES

1 *Asian Development Outlook* 2000, Oxford University Press, 2000.
2 Prof. Tommy Koh, Executive Director of the Asia-Europe Foundation, *Sunday Times*, Singapore, 9 April 1999.
3 This, of course, is not to deny that there are other security challenges as well, including non-conventional transnational ones like crime and the narcotics trade.
4 *Far Eastern Economic Review*, 23 December 1999.
5 See 'Can Japan find its voice?, *The Economist*, 6 May 2000.
6 For a description of some of the strains in US-Japan relations and their effects on the alliance see Christopher B. Johnstone, 'Strained Alliance: US-Japan Diplomacy in the Asian Financial Crisis, in *Survival*, Summer 1999, Vol. 41, No. 2.
7 The figures cited here are from the *Military Balance 1999-2000*, of The International Institute of Strategic Studies, Oxford University Press, 1999.

PART FOUR

CREATING A EURASIAN RESEARCH CULTURE

CHAPTER 10

ASEM: TIME FOR AN OVERHAUL

NURIA OFKEN

ASEM 2 in London 1998 was overshadowed by the financial crisis in Asia, which had broken out only a few months before the summit meeting. For this reason and because of the fact that the ASEM process had up to this point still been a comparatively young dialogue forum, a critical evaluation of the outcomes of the ASEM co-operation as well as of its procedural structure was not carried out. Shortly after the Bangkok summit, the ASEM process experienced a considerable proliferation of projects mainly in the field of economic co-operation and in the realm of cultural exchange. But already before the London summit the process seemed to have lost momentum so that one of the results of ASEM 2 was the establishment of a Vision Group to examine possible fields of future co-operation. From a results-oriented perspective, the latest after the London summit, the dialogue forum lost much of its vitality and today, it seems to be almost paralysed. Has the process of creating closer ties between the two regions already surpassed its zenith? This article presents the view that, even though the Asian crises may have had some effects on ASEM, it is mainly both structural deficits within the ASEM co-operation and the different stages of economic development among its members that lame the process. Furthermore, if ASEM did not possess a hidden agenda parallel to the existing official one, regular misperceptions from within as well as from outside ASEM regarding its function and effectiveness could be avoided.

THE LONDON SUMMIT AND AFTER

How have the three pillars of ASEM (political, economic and financial, and cultural and technical co-operation) developed? In London political dialogue did not play a significant role. Especially concerning security issues the division between ASEM-members was - and, to date, still is - so great that it has become habitual to assign political dialogue to a list of suggestions made by senior officials previously. Seemingly they provide an indispensable handicap to the third pillar. To this end, senior officials meet several times ahead of every summit to decide upon those subjects, which can be assessed as opportune for the leaders' discussion. With regard to the London venue, they agreed on the appropriateness of subjects such as the Korean Peninsula, Bosnia, Kosovo, and Cambodia. In fact, political leaders took up their proposals. Strikingly some of the Asian political leaders gathered in London showed a strong determination to discuss European problems like the situation in Yugoslavia vividly whereas they refrained from commenting frankly on sensitive issues concerning Asian security. But this was not the only point of imbalance in political dialogue. Enlargement of ASEM, which can be seen as a part of the political dialogue, was, and still is, one of the ongoing points of dispute within ASEM. For the EU new membership in ASEAN does not automatically imply participation in ASEM. Renewed human rights violations and violent oppression of the opposition there caused the EU to oppose any participation of Myanmar in ASEM or EU-ASEAN meetings strongly. Both sides were unable to agree on how to treat the membership-issue (applications for admissions have been submitted by Russia, Pakistan, India, Australia, New Zealand, and others). The Chairman's Statement (CS) of London simply states that 'enlargement should be conducted on the basis of consensus by the Heads of State and Government' meaning that one single veto can block new membership.[1] Specially from the NGO perspective, political dialogue at ASEM 2 was a disappointment since human rights were not even mentioned in the second Chairman's Statement in contrast to the one issued on the occasion of ASEM 1.

The overarching subject during the summit was of course the financial crisis in East Asia. Disparate views among Asians and Europeans evolved around the role of the International Monetary Fund (IMF) as well as around the need for domestic reform. Unlike human rights organizations which underlined the need for fundamental political reform in East Asia, European politicians first and foremost lay emphasis on the necessity of structural reform in the financial sector of the affected countries. Neither Europeans nor Asians disagreed with the fact that reform of the banking sector was imperative in principle, but they differed in their views on the cause of the financial crisis. On the Asian side some politicians were convinced that unrestricted currency speculation and rapid flow of investment capital was the root of the crisis. Europeans for their part were convinced that the financial policies in the affected countries had to be seen as the main reason for the economic troubles. Regarding the immense problems they had been facing since summer 1997, Asians expected additional financial support from the EU. But the EU leaders took the stance that the IMF and the World Bank should handle the crisis. The ASEM Trust Fund unilaterally suggested by host, Tony Blair, with the objective of providing technical assistance and training in both the financial and social sectors for Asia was more a gesture of good will. Not even all-European ASEM members joined it. As the Trust Fund, which is to be administered by the World Bank, only attracted pledges of some US$40 million, it was considered to be of a more symbolic nature. Furthermore, the EU insisted that Asians should abide by the IMF prescriptions for economic and financial reform and did not support the Japanese idea of an Asian Monetary Fund (AMF).

Economic co-operation for both European and Asian governments seemed, from the beginning, to be the main purpose of ASEM. To this end, several task forces, working-groups, experts-groups, shepherds'-groups and the like were established and assigned to work out and implement action plans on trade facilitation, customs co-operation, and the promotion of investment. At the London summit the Trade Facilitation Action Plan (TFAP) including the reduction of non-tariff trade barriers was adopted. But the Asian refusal to accept timetables diluted the fence of TFAP. In the field of foreign investment disagreement over intellectual property rights caused a stumbling block in the implementation of the Investment Promotion Action Plan (IPAP), which was also adopted. Important trade issues like anti-dumping measures and GSP were conspicuously absent from the summit agenda. And even though in London ASEM members once again hastened to stress compatibility with WTO agreements, participants refrained from taking steps to accelerate the implementation of the agreements of the Uruguay round.

In a nutshell, the London summit can be called neither a real success nor an outright failure. Europeans managed to convey their Asians counterparts the message of solidarity and strong interest. Asians could be convinced by Europeans that Europe would not close its markets to Asian exports - there would be no *fortress Europe*. Asians for their part, gave assurances that they would resist protectionism and honour free trade and market liberalization.

FROM ASEM 2 TO ASEM 3

Since the summit the most important happenings at the political level have been a meeting of Finance Ministers in January 1999, of Foreign Ministers in March 1999, and of Ministers of Trade and Industry in October 1999. Both the meetings of Foreign Ministers and that of the Ministers of Trade and Industry marked low points in the Euro-Asian relationship. Whereas political dialogue has always been a difficult field in ASEM right from its inception, it seemed as if economic co-operation had got off to a better start. This was a false hope and at the ASEM Trade and Industry meeting in Berlin, Ministers did not manage to find a common language in which to discuss WTO related issues. The meeting was dominated by discussions of new global trade liberalization talks and the Ministers disagreed on the scope of any new round and on whether it should include any reference to labour standards. This controversial issue was and still is promoted by many Europeans and resisted by many in Asia. The only small success at the Trade and Industry Ministers meeting was the launch of a website called *Virtual Exchange* designed to provide information on national investment promotion websites of ASEM members, as well as information on the IPAP.[2] Another gathering worth mentioning since ASEM 2 in London is the fourth Asia-Europe Business Forum (AEBF) held from September to October 1999, a few days prior to the Trade and Industry Economic Ministers' encounter. The next one will take place in Seoul shortly before ASEM 3. Taken altogether, between April 1998 and March 2000 more than about twenty-five meetings at expert level and senior official level were held, ten of them devoted to the TFAP.[3] Even though a practical approach to reducing non-tariff barriers was chosen after their adoption at the London summit, neither the TFAP nor the IPAP has yet made any substantial progress.

Political dialogue has from the outset regularly caused diplomatic dissonance between Asians and Europeans. One repeatedly discussed issue was the quarrel between Portugal and Indonesia over East Timor. At the last Foreign Ministers' meeting in Berlin in March 1999 under the German EU presidency, human rights as well as the situation in East Timor were officially placed on the agenda. Allegedly, the German Foreign Minister, Joschka Fischer, circulated a paper containing information on human rights abuses in East Asia.[4] Not surprisingly, the meeting was not a success from the Asian perspective. Before the meeting Asians were worried about whether Europeans might have lost interest in their region. The poor attendance by their European colleagues seemed to confirm their fears. Only ten out of fifteen European Ministers came to the meeting.[5] To exacerbate the situation even more the EU and ASEAN failed to reach a compromise on the treatment of Myanmar. An informal meeting between the EU and ASEAN scheduled to have taken place after the Foreign Ministers' meeting was cancelled because some Europeans were reluctant to sit at the same table as Myanmar. One positive result of the Foreign Ministers meeting was the presentation of the Vision Group report which addresses medium and long-term perspectives for Asia-Europe relations.[6] The Vision Group delivered nine 'major recommendations' and twenty-two 'other recommendations' in the fields of economic co-operation, environmental co-operation, educational, cultural and societal exchanges, as well as promoting political and security co-operation.

Turning to co-operation in the cultural and technical domain, the widening of the scope of activities has steadily been set in motion. A variety of initiatives have been taken by ASEM members. Think tanks have formed a network called 'Council for Asia-Europe Co-operation' (CAEC). CAEC is an independent initiative by twelve think-tanks in Europe and Asia (including Australia) which aims at facilitating co-operation among policy specialists and at enhancing discussions on the future direction of Asia-European relations.[7] It was set up in 1996, shortly after Bangkok. In the environmental sector the Asia-Europe Environment Technology Centre (AEETC) officially opened its doors in March 1999 (coincidental with the second Foreign Ministers meeting in Berlin) in Bangkok with the aim at promoting co-operation in environmental and R&D activities. The establishment of the Asia-Europe Centre at the University of Malaya, which was upgraded in January 2000 and is now called Asia-Europe Institute (AEI) aims at fostering exchanges of students and scholars from both regions. By organizing a notable number of symposia, seminars, and workshops the Asia-Europe Foundation (ASEF) in Singapore has taken, without doubt, a crucial role in advancing the third pillar. Since its launch in February 1997, it has organized more than fifty activities including seminars on human rights, ASEF cultural forums, summer schools, cultural managers training, seminars for journalists, cultural festivals, and the like. The data-bank *Intellectual Exchange Inventory* contains information on institutions, projects, conferences, and other initiatives that are useful to intellectual exchanges between the two regions.[8] With a distinct focus on high-level interchange, ASEF has successfully promoted the gradual expansion of inter-regional contacts and represents the driving force behind the pillar cultural and intellectual co-operation.

CHARACTERISTICS

In ASEM, political dialogue is conducted by Foreign Ministers and the leaders and prepared and maintained through the meetings of senior officials' meetings (SOM), which are subjected to less public scrutiny. At this level, issues are dealt with informally, in open but inconclusive discussions. Political dialogue has undergone a particular development, which is often overseen by the public, and if recognized, it is often underestimated. Certain issues, so called delicate issues pertaining to political dialogue such as human rights, labour relations, and good governance, have been shifted from the level of high politicians to the sphere of workshops and seminars.[9] This means that these issues have not been abandoned in ASEM, but are not dealt with at the top or at key bureaucratic level. European attempts to bring the so called sensitive issues into play as an *official* part of gatherings on a higher level (which was for example the case on the occasion of the last Foreign Ministers meeting in Berlin) are an exception. This tendency explains why human rights have been omitted in the last Chairman's Statement and why neither human rights organizations nor the people's forum are heard in ASEM.[10] Unfortunately there is a broadly shared perspective that since the London summit the ASEM-process lost its dynamic and its weight as an interregional forum designed to complete the weak link between Asia and Europe in the 'global triangle'. This assumption is true in so far as the fact that activities in the economic pillar may have not necessarily decreased in sum but have stagnated in progress. For those proponents who hold up economic co-operation as the flagship of ASEM, the dialogue forum has indeed faded into the realm of insignificance.

The ASEM process is a mixture of a top-down approach juxtaposed with the idea of integrating private networks into the new relationship. In this construction, it provides different layers of contact. There are biannual gatherings of heads of state and government as well as meetings of foreign, trade and industry, and finance ministers and meetings of senior officials. Summit meetings with their catalytic effect are the culmination points of the ASEM process. At a lower level, civil servants, academics, students, think-tanks, business-people and young parliamentarians are involved in the process in order to foster dialogue in their respective field of engagement. Here the principal aim is to start up a wide network linking non-governmental actors in the private and public sphere in the economic domain respectively with the business sector as well as with the cultural or civil society fields. The key characteristic of the summits, their informality, is designed to provide the opportunity for an open exchange of views between the heads of state. In the obligatory Chairman's Statement issued after every summit there are no individual positions identifiable. Hence negotiation, the elaboration of a legally binding agenda, or even a formal institutionalization of the co-operation are not provided for in ASEM. It is largely perceived as a consultative forum and co-operation such as the implementation of follow-up measures is based on consent. This informality engenders a certain flexibility: flexibility in the choice of the partners with whom an activity can be implemented as well as flexibility regarding the subject of a project to be tackled. Consequently the open nature of the procedural structure of ASEM helps generate a variety of channels through which certain problems can be dealt with and provides the occasion to 'move issues up and down a hierarchy depending on their importance and sensitivity.'[11]

ASEM is an institution *sui generis* and as such it does not fit into a commonly held utilitarian-rationalist view on why states engage in international institutions.[12] ASEM is not an international organization because it is not based on any legally obligating rules - it does not even have a secretariat. Nor is it an international regime, for it is not based on 'implicit or explicit principles, norms, rules, and decision-making procedures [...] in a given area of international relations.'[13] The concept of ASEM is based mainly on the so-called *Asian way*: priority is placed on consent, on voluntary assumption of obligations, and on non-interference, thus avoiding every kind of constraint that could arise from a previously negotiated set of binding rules. Nevertheless, it has to be seen as an institution because it provides regular and co-ordinated interregional mechanisms of co-operation between states.[14] If we were to consider the ASEM process as a specific institution in a rationalist sense consisting of a 'persistent and connected sets of rules (formal or informal) that prescribe behavioural roles, constrain activity, and shape expectations' designed to improve co-operation between states, then ASEM would fall short.[15] According to the logic of the widespread rationalist belief, co-operation depends first and foremost on interest calculations. States are seen as utility-maximizers so that no shared norms, values, idealism, or altruism are seen as necessary to actors to set off a process of co-operation. Consequently an actor's motivation is primarily guided by rational motives and is based on the premise that if there were no potential gains to be had from multilateral co-operation, there would be no need for the creation of an international institution. Even though co-operation may (at times) be more advantageous for one party than for the other, it is still assumed to have additional value for both parties, for example, in reducing transaction costs.

Bearing in mind these basic assumptions about why states engage in membership of an international institution it becomes obvious that ASEM cannot easily be compared to an institution in the sense described above since dialogue instead of results-oriented co-operation is officially defined as being the major constituent of ASEM. Although the process was labelled 'partnership for greater growth' one reason for its weakness is the absence of a clear and well-defined set of concrete policy goals in each of the three pillars.[16] The first as well as the second Chairman's Statement reveal that there was, and in part still is, no strong will among some ASEM members to streamline ASEM activities. It is for the sake of informality that the whole process is not given a clearly defined direction. An update of the Asia-Europe Co-operation Framework (AECF) to be adopted at ASEM 3 in Seoul is charted precisely to sharpen co-operation. Significantly, priorities set out in the AECF are vigorously disputed though they would indeed be helpful for the future development of the ASEM process.

The underlying rationale which the initiators of ASEM seem to adhere to was not that of a strategically calculating actor who seeks to bargain by efficient co-operation. Otherwise the first CS would have presented more specified ideas, for example on how to strengthen co-operation in the economic field. When it comes to informality ASEM even confronts us with a paradox. On the one hand, the openness and vagueness of the ASEM-agenda laid down by the CS enables its multidimensionality regarding the issues picked up along the way as well as its relatively impressive proliferation of projects and initiatives in quantitative terms. In ASEM, states are subject to almost no kind of formal prescription that would legally force them to comply with a common rule. But this does not mean that everyone has a free choice either. With respect to enlargement, for example, the principle of consent hugely limits the will of each actor to push for his favourite candidate as a new member. So, on the other hand, the prevailing practice of political non-interference and of consent derived from the superordinated principle of sovereignty often hinders ASEM members from becoming active in their individual field of interest. In short, the lack of obligating rules helps to widen the thematic spectrum for co-operation but at the same time clearly restricts it.

Another characteristic of ASEM is the persistent emphasis on the cultural distance between the people of the two regions.[17] It serves as an explanation of why ASEM needs to be in first place a dialogue forum, and why it should prioritize enhancement of understanding and communication among Asians and Europeans. Before we enter into negotiation, so the argument goes, we need to get to know each other better. In view of this modest claim, one is tempted to conclude that expecting tangible outcomes or a certain measurable output would appear to be an improper attitude to adopt towards ASEM.

In reality, however, Europeans as well as Asians would not be reluctant to convert ASEM into a forum for substantial co-operation. This is a phenomenon, which is referred to here as ASEM's hidden agenda. There can be no doubt that ASEM is designed merely as a consultative forum. This is its official side. Yet, undeniably ASEM members seek to negotiate. And they do so bilaterally rather than collectively. The only problem is that actors in ASEM have highly diverging interests and expectations. As a result, their different views on what can be considered a fertile co-operation lead to different priorities in objectives. Several *ad-hoc* alliances between single European and Asian states within ASEM have shown that the preferences of all the twenty-six members are difficult to reconcile. Given their vastly different levels of economic development and political systems, it is also difficult to deepen the institution with the help of devices like the AECF. So besides the structure of the ASEM-process, it is also the different stages of economic development, particularly salient on the Asian side, which are responsible for the different expectations members of ASEM possess. The donor-recipient mindset between Europe and some East Asian countries has still not been overcome, although the frequent repetition of the 'partnership between equals' phrase is intended to convey the impression of a relationship that is not aid-based. Several ASEM activities reflect this problematic, in general those projects dealing with infrastructure development, energy, technology, and environmental issues.

IN THE LONG RUN ...

Without doubt, ASEM needs a re-definition of its goals. The already perceptible shift in ASEM illustrates that in the future, focusing on the third pillar would be the most promising perspective under the given circumstances. A sharpening of the ASEM agenda would elicit a more honest, and at the same time, more realistic setting for the ASEM process. More honest in the sense that it has to be recognized that Asians, especially Southeast Asians, and Europeans, as their disputes about WTO-related issues demonstrate, have in fact diverging priorities concerning economic co-operation. More realistically, because experience gained so far shows that even a practical approach in economic co-operation is doomed to failure or at least to irrelevance. Turning to political dialogue, up to now it has at no time played any decisive role in ASEM in the sense that Europeans and Asians would have agreed on at least one common standpoint concerning international politics. There is not the slightest hint that in the future, it will become a meaningful part of the ASEM process. In the eyes of the public, political dialogue is non-existent. Where it appears to take place (e.g. at the last Foreign Ministers meeting) contention between Europeans and Asians arises. At the level where it is largely maintained, it is far away from the public eye, so that enhancing mutual understanding through political dialogue is restricted to fostering understanding between senior officials.

The ASEM process has already undergone a specific development that shows what the right direction could be: a clear focus on the third pillar. Unless ASEM remains a purely informal dialogue forum, cultural and intellectual exchange seems to be the most auspicious way to set up a new quality in the relationship between Asians and Europeans.

NOTES

1 See Introduction of the Chairman's Statement: The second Asia-Europe Meeting, London 3-4 April 1998.
2 See: http://europa.eu.int/comm/external_relations/asem_ipap_vie/texts/-links.htm, 02.06.00. In addition ASEM Connect (http://www.asem-connect.com.sg/welco, 02.06.00.) can be consulted from business people for information on investment opportunities.
3 Figures taken from 'ASEM Companion' at the website of the Asia-Europe Foundation. The ASEF websites provide an excellent overview over the ASEM process. See: http://www.asef.org.
4 Bersick, Sebastian: ASEM 2000 – Das dritte Asia-Europe Meeting in Seoul und die Rolle von Nicht-Regierungsorganisationen, in: http://-www.asienhaus.de/publikat/korea/kofo2-99/asem2000.htm, 28.02.00.
5 *The Straits Times*, 30 March 1999.
6 The report is published in http://www.mofat.go.kr/aevg, 02.06.00.
7 Council for Asia-Europe Cooperation: The Rationale and Common Agenda for Asia-Europe Cooperation, Japan Centre for International Exchange, Tokyo 1997.
8 Figures taken from the ASEF-Homepage. Other ASEM-websites: CORDIS is a website relating to ASEM science and technology co-operation (http://www.cordis.lu/asem/, 02.06.00). The so called Resource Centre is the website of the Asia-Europe Child initiative. It provides information for those who fight against sexual abuse and exploitation of children. See: http:/www.asem.org/, 02.06.00.
9 ASEF for example has organized a meeting on labour relations in Oct. 98, a colloquium on human rights and human responsibility in Nov. 98 and second informal ASEM seminar on human rights in Beijing in June 99.
10 The ASEM 2000 people's forum is an alternative NGO summit, which will be held 18-21 October 2000 at the margins of ASEM 3. For more information see: http://www.oneworld.net/anydoc.cgi?url=http://www.-tni.org/asia/watch/asem50.htm, 15.07.00.
11 Forster, Anthony: Continuity and change in turbulent times, in: *International Affairs*, 75 (1999) 4, 743-58, p. 753.
12 Keeping with Robert Koehane's definition, rationalist thought encompasses realist and neo-liberal ideology. See Robert Keohane, International Institutions: Two approaches, in: Robert O. Keohane: *International Institutions and State Power*, Boulder, 1989, 158-79, p. 160.
13 Stephen Krasner: Structural Causes and Regime Consequences: Regimes as Intervening Variables, in: Stephen Krasner: *International Regimes*, Cornell University Press, 1983, p. 2.

14 Julie Gilson underlines the impact that co-ordination among ASEM partners can have. According to her mechanisms of co-ordination have constructive effects on intra-regional integration in East Asia. See Gilson, Julie: Japan's role in the Asia-Europe Meeting. Establishing an inter-regional or intraregional agenda?, in: *Asian Survey*, 39 (1999) 5, 736-52.

15 Keohane (1989): 163.

16 See Chapter: Towards a common vision for Asia and Europe, in the Chairman's Statement of the Asia-Europe Meeting, Bangkok 2 March 1996.

17 David Bobrow identifies a dominant pattern of recognition of differences and points out that, 'throughout the history of ASEM, Asians and Europeans have been aware of their differences'. See David B. Bobrow: The US and ASEM: why the hegemon didn't bark, in: *The Pacific Review*, 12 (1999) 1, 103-28, p. 110-11.

CHAPTER 11

THE NEED FOR AN ASEM RESEARCH PLATFORM

SABINE KUYPERS AND WIM STOKHOF

The Programme for Europe-Asia Research Linkages (PEARL) is a network of researchers from Asia and Europe, representing leading Asian and European Studies Institutes in the field of the Humanities and Social Sciences. PEARL was established in Seoul in October 1998 under the patronage of the European Science Foundation Asia Committee (ESF-AC, Strasbourg), and the Asia-Europe Foundation (ASEF, Singapore). PEARL is an open network. Its members belong to the ASEM countries.

PEARL was established out of a need felt on both Asian and European sides for research interaction between the two regions, and out of a sense of opportunity created by the gathering of strength of the ASEM process and the establishment of ASEF. PEARL members are concerned that research may not yet receive the attention it deserves on the agenda of ASEM. PEARL is a broad-based research partnership encompassing the Humanities and Social Sciences of the Eurasian continent, which is poised to deliver great intellectual benefits to scholarship at national, regional, and global levels. Promotion of this partnership ought to be an integral part of the ASEM dynamic and a major element in the activities of the ASEF.

PEARL has set its sights on developing a Eurasian research culture. The most effective tool for tightening links between Asia and Europe is to develop long-term joint Asia-Europe research projects on a multilateral basis. This will not only enrich the quality of research, but will enable attention to be directed more effectively to issues that are pertinent to both Asia and Europe.

A joint initiative, PEARL promotes and initiates studies of contemporary developments in Asia and Europe in a comparative perspective and against their historical and cultural backgrounds. It seeks to integrate the best of the European Studies and Asian Studies and to provide an institutional framework for collaboration on topics of common interest.

So far within the existing relevant bodies such as the ASEM or the ASEF, no substantial possibilities yet exist to develop and implement joint multilateral Asia-Europe research and educational programmes. PEARL thus provides a unique structure for Asia-Europe co-operation in the field of research. PEARL does what others do, but more pertinently cannot do.

THE NEED FOR RESEARCH IN ASEM

The emergence of formal Europe-Asia links through the ASEM process is an important step in the history of the Eurasian continent. The era of European colonialism in Asia ended four to five decades ago. Since then relations between the two regions have been relatively distant and fragmentary. This state of affairs was able to prevail so long because of the aftermath of the colonial legacy, the Cold War, and the overwhelming political, economic, and cultural presence of the US in both Asia and Europe.

After the fall of the Berlin Wall, international relations changed radically. Europe-Asia relations strengthened and seizing the opportunity the ASEM process is now beginning to establish a partnership between the two regions on an unprecedented basis of parity. The rub is that ASEM has been devised primarily to address economic, political, and security issues. Research is blatantly absent from its agenda whereas multilateral research and education are the most essential tools by which to reinforce an Asia-Europe rapprochement. Therefore PEARL emphasizes the importance of an intellectual partnership that also pays attention to cultural co-operation.

Research linkages between Asia and Europe, especially in the Humanities and Social Sciences, have remained relatively weak since the end of the colonial era, in particular when compared with the contacts between both regions and the US. Many Asian scholars continue to work within the scientific paradigms acquired during their studies in the US, whereas European scholars have tended to be academically self-sufficient.

Although each side has much to offer the other, the construction of a durable relationship, which deals in more than goods and services will require careful attention being paid to Europe-Asian interaction in the world of ideas. Because the rapprochement between Asia and Europe has been rapid, decision makers and the general public in both regions still rely on obsolete cultural stereotypes.

These stereotypes were perhaps adequate in the days when contexts were sparse, but they are inadequate to deal with, and at times indeed actively damaging to, the complex, multifaceted relationship between Asia and Europe which has emerged in the final decade of the twentieth century. The global communications revolution gives the misleading impression that the rapid delivery of information brings with it immediate understanding. In fact, rapid communication tends to reinforce the use of stereotypes as an easy tool for sorting abundant information. PEARL provides a framework for replacing stereotypes with operative solutions based on recent comparative research.

RESEARCH AS AN INTEGRATING FORCE

An important part of seeking a solution is the development of a Eurasian research culture in the Humanities and Social Sciences. It is an inescapable fact that each of the national participants in the process works with distinctive national research paradigms, and each of these systems has both strengths and weaknesses. To the extent that ASEM participants take part in international research projects - and this extent varies greatly from country to country - that research is often linked to paradigmatic approaches developed in the US. The research preoccupations of the US are not alien to those of the rest of the world, but neither are they entirely congruent with those of Asia and Europe.

Without relinquishing existing research links with the US, complementary research cultures which are more attuned to Eurasian interests should be developed. While national boundaries are disappearing from the economic map, the need to understand the factors that shape a regional or national culture becomes more pressing. Culture is not just a matter of heritage and history, but also an integral part of our daily lives. It is a reality upon which progress, including economic growth and welfare depends.

It would be extremely timely to enrich the process of Europe-Asia rapprochement with research programmes in the Humanities and Social Sciences. Long-term joint research programmes in these sciences will deepen our understanding of respective cultural backgrounds. They will serve to ensure peaceful co-existence, meaningful and productive integration, and lasting co-operation. They will also enhance a much-needed mutual understanding. Needless to say, they will encourage people-to-people contact and create links and networks based on trust and mutual respect. We should not be blind to the fact that the academic and sociological character of Asian and European Studies varies enormously, depending partly on colonial experiences, overall academic cultures, and current political perceptions. Research both builds on and reacts against past experiences of conquest and domination. Researchers are located in many different kinds of institutions, with very differently defined mandates and levels of funding; and scholarly rubrics such as 'Asia', 'Europe', 'Social Sciences', and 'Humanities' enjoy widely varying status, both in national scholarly communities and in the eyes of policy-makers.

THE EUROPEAN SCIENCE FOUNDATION AND THE ASIA-EUROPE FOUNDATION

The work of the European Science Foundation (ESF) has not only shown the scope for encouraging a European research culture in various fields it has also highlighted some of the practical difficulties involved in achieving it. Ineluctably it has clearly demonstrated the importance and value of the multilateral endeavours taking place within its framework.

The establishment of a European research culture that compliments and stands alongside the various national research cultures is a way of ensuring that issues spanning the continent, receive the best possible analytical attention. This rich European experience can be used to develop a Eurasian research culture in which issues of common interest can come to the fore. More important still are the ideas, analyses, and solutions that can be drawn from the various research cultures in Europe and Asia.

A research culture of this kind may directly engage the efforts of a couple of thousand scholars across the ASEM community. The spin off from their endeavours can be enormous. It derives its influence on the one hand through the formulation and analysis of the issues that move governments and the media and on the other hand through the students trained and educated in this culture who move outside academia to other positions in society. The cost of developing and sustaining such a research culture represents a small financial investment in comparison to the fruits that might be derived from it.

The work of the ESF was hampered by the fact that the Humanities and the Social Sciences were included relatively late within its field of operations. In 1994, only about 15 per cent of the budget allocated to specific scientific programmes and networks went to the Humanities and Social Sciences. Now the institutions of the ASEM process are taking shape it is important to seek ways of incorporating the Humanities and Social Sciences into the process from the very beginning so that they too can have productive influence on ASEM proceedings.

At the inaugural summit of the ASEM in 1996, the objective of the ASEF was stated as: 'To enhance mutual understanding between Asia and Europe, through greater intellectual, cultural and people-to-people exchanges.' Given its brief and restricted funding possibilities, ASEF concentrates on short-term activities only. In its intellectual exchange programme ASEF stimulates academic discourse. It supports the *Education Hub Programme* as proposed at the second ASEM in London in 1998. Notwithstanding the useful initiatives taken by ASEF, we believe it necessary that ASEM should pay more structural and long-term attention to joint research and education as two major elements in a (cultural) rapprochement between the two regions. Initiating and implementing joint multilateral research could play an important role in achieving ASEF's objectives.

EUROPEAN COMMISSION AND NETWORKS IN ASIA

The importance of creating links between Asian and European universities was stressed at the Bangkok summit. Disappointedly, so far, the activities of the EC in the field of the Humanities and Social Sciences research have, been very much limited. The Fifth Framework Programme (FP5) shows a clear interest in research. A closer look reveals that this interest is focused mainly on problem-solving work, technology, and science. The aim of the FP5 is defined as to help EU companies to meet challenges of the twenty-first century and, through research, to come up with answers to a wide range of issues that are important for European society.

Clearly, this attitude is too Europe-focused to be instrumental in the general Asia-Europe dialogue. Fortunately, some bilateral initiatives in the field of joint Asia-Europe research have been taken (EU-India, EU-China). In programmes in which bilateral research is carried out, this is often focused on such important topics as policy issues, trade, finance, strategic issues and the like. Topics that contribute to a better insight into each other's way of thinking and behaviour, which are so essential to a better mutual understanding, are not given the attention they deserve.

The degree of national and regional institution building in the Asian ASEM member countries is still at a very early stage. Although on several occasions member states have stressed the importance of national and regional co-operative links, for several reasons this co-operation has developed at a very low pace. Cross-national professorial associations such as the European ones (e.g. the European Association for Chinese Studies, the European Association for South East Asian Studies) are still at the teething stage. One positive development is the introduction of the ASEAN University Network (AUN) in 1995. Here some ten universities signed an agreement on co-operation between ASEAN scholars, pertaining to developing human resources, plus the dissemination and exchange of scholarly knowledge. Other networks are the Association of Southeast Asian Institutions of Higher Learning (ASAIHL), the Association of Universities in Asia and the Pacific (AUAP), and the University Mobility in Asia and the Pacific (UMAP). These activities, however, are not focused on joint collaborative research programmes.

TOWARDS AN ASEM RESEARCH PLATFORM

ASEM is a unique mechanism for dialogue. It is an informal process and it has no permanent organizational body. This poses a problem because if certain programmes, beneficial to the ultimate aim of the ASEM (co-operation in the economic, political, and cultural fields) are to be implemented successfully, they need an organizational structure. This has been done in a few cases. Specific institutions or programmes, which were created on the basis of ASEM decisions, are: the ASEF; the Asia-Europe Environment and Technology Centre (AEETC), of which the objective is the promotion of Asia-Europe co-operation on environmental issues; and the ASEM trust Fund, which has been set up to promote technical assistance and training in financial and social sectors for Asian countries damaged by the recent financial crisis. Now, the need is urgently being felt by different parties and at various levels for an ASEM Research Platform which will be specifically designed to encourage multilateral scientific co-operation at an Asia-Europe level.

Three major reasons for seeking a top-level presence of Asian and European Studies in the ASEM process can be identified. First, the need for a creative and well-informed policy on both the European and Asian sides has in many cases outrun the capacity of government administrations to deliver it. The Asia-Europe rapprochement has caught officials and policy-makers across a wide range of fields unprepared. The perceptions of Asia of European officials and politicians precisely like these of their counterparts' perceptions of Europe, are often restricted, blurred by historical reminiscences and time constraints, or the one or the other, which prevent officials from specializing in certain fields and areas. These are busy people who are sometimes forced to rely on aphorisms and stereotypes as tools for ordering the complex new world in which they find themselves. As the policy-making apparatus at the ASEM level grows, there needs to be a visible Asian and European Studies presence at the same level to ensure that officials and policy-makers can quickly lay their hands on the best advice on complex inter-regional issues.

The second major reason is the need for cross-national co-operation. The distinctive national traditions of research and scholarship in various aspects of Asian and European Studies which exist throughout the ASEM community are a precious resource. In the present environment of globalization, however, these traditions need to be brought together into complementary partnerships. No single nation can sustain a research endeavour on the scale needed to address the issues arising form globalization fully; co-operation and collaboration offer the only solution.

The work of the ESF Asia Committee has shown that internationally oriented bodies can play a major stimulating role both in bringing small centres of excellence out of isolation and in promoting innovative research which would not normally find support within any single national framework. By bringing Asian and European studies in Asia and Europe into a facilitating framework, it will be possible to create further creative synergies without in any way detracting from the current strengths of the national research efforts.

The third cogent reason is the need to link academia to the ASEM process. The reason for acting now is that the key institutions for ASEM co-operation are in the process of formation. Long-term joint research projects, on a multilateral basis, are a most effective tool for reinforcing links between Asia and Europe. Especially in the Asian context, these long-term ventures are conditions for sustainable success. Experience has proven that such personal relationships, once established, continue to thrive, even after the project has finished. The Humanities and Social Sciences are particularly important in this respect. They form an integrating force by contributing to a better insight into each other's political, social, and economic concepts and in the way in which parties cope with issues of common interest.

We propose that, in the near future, ASEM member states finance an ASEM/PEARL pilot research project and establish an ASEM Research Platform in 2002. In its 1999 report *For a Better Tomorrow. Asia-Europe Partnership in the 21st Century*, the Vision Group stresses the importance of co-operation in education and exchange programmes. This is an important and necessary step forward.

The ASEM Research Platform should monitor and implement co-operative activities in research. This platform should be an umbrella organization for the wide range of high-quality scientific research in general and could consist of representatives from major research institutions from both continents. It should be committed to promoting high quality science at a Eurasian level. In this platform Asia and Europe can work closely together on topics of common interest. Research agendas and strategies will be designed and developed by a number of committees in which renowned scholars from Asia and Europe can participate. It should be funded by the ASEM member states.

Scientific work to be sponsored by the platform should not be restricted to the Humanities and Socials Sciences, but it should also stimulate joint research in the medical sciences, the life and environmental sciences, and the natural sciences and engineering. Needless to say, the ASEM Research Platform will have to work closely with already existing bodies such as the ASEF, the AEETC, and with possible projects of e.g. the EC and those resulting from initiatives as proposed by the Vision Group.

The establishment of an ASEM Research Platform in close co-operation with, or under the aegis of ASEF, would remedy the overemphasis in ASEM on trade and security issues. It will facilitate the Asian members in developing a region-wide counterpart organization for the ESF, which could function as a window on Asia for foreign scholars. A feasibility study on an ASEM research platform is the logical next step.

CHAPTER 12

TOWARDS A VIRTUAL ASEM:
FROM INFORMATION TO KNOWLEDGE

CÉSAR DE PRADO YEPES

The rapid evolution in information and communications technologies over the past two years has raised hopes that they will soon become affordable to more and more people and help solve some of the most pressing economic problems the world is facing in the new millennium. Indeed, techno-optimism grew as the turn of the year 2000 brought a renewed wave of corporate dynamism rather than generalized software malfunctions. Yet, techno-pessimists rightly point out how globalization has increased uncertainty and inequality, partly aggravated by info-communications technologies as software viruses keep attacking computer systems, and electronic commerce and content impinge on valuable traditions.

These developments are reflected in the evolution of the ASEM process. By the time of the third summit in October 2000, scores of ASEM-related activities will have developed in a climate of openness and flexibility. Yet, the growing number of partially divergent interests raises some uncertainty about their future evolution. Nevertheless, I argue that it may be possible to find ways to strengthen ASEM visions by profiting from the positive aspects of important trends in global info-communications. In the following sections, while commenting on recent global and ASEM developments in telecommunications infrastructure, information technology, content and culture, governance and education, I shall propose avenues of development that will eventually converge to keep the positive momentum that has developed out of the mesh of bilateral economic and political relations between both regions.

KEEP LINKING BASIC INFRASTRUCTURES

As travellers from London to Seoul may choose between several complementary means of transportation and alternative routes, electronic information bits travelling between ASEM countries can take different paths and roam through alternative infrastructures inter-linked by various types of hardware and software technologies. But, although the number of direct links and overall network capacity keeps growing with the new generation of undersea fibre optic cables and satellite-based networks, it is likely they will again face congestion in the oncoming interactive multimedia environment, thus forcing ASEM bits to take longer and maybe more costly paths.

To ensure ready communications access ASEM heads will have to agree to give substance to the various co-operation proposals that have been put forward in the past. At the time of the London Summit, a broad proposal for an Asia-Europe Information Technology and Telecommunications Programme to be co-ordinated from Bangkok was presented to eventually promote co-operation in areas like education, health care, cultural exchanges and research and development. A year later, young leaders meeting in Seoul suggested establishing a direct information superhighway network between Asia and Europe that would open into many opportunities for co-operation. Commendably, and as part of a series of proposals to enhance key bilateral and ASEM relations in various economic, technological, educational and cultural fields, Korean president, Kim Dae-Jung, reached a tentative agreement in France last March to develop a 'Trans-Eurasia e-Network' or 'millennium global project' for the connection of Europe and Asia in stages with a super high-speed telecommunications network. The idea is to start linking the growing trans-European network of research institutes with its Korean and Asia-Pacific counterparts, and not too much later to extend this to link with initiatives in Europe and Asia to develop full-fledged information societies.

To achieve such an objective, technological standards have to remain largely open and compatible, assuring better interconnection and interoperability of mutual infrastructures. This is still possible as new generations of wireless mobile communications with Internet browsing capabilities are being broadly implemented. The GSM family of standards has been widely adopted in Europe and Asia, and the new UMTS generation with Internet access capacities is being implemented in Japan and Europe, representing the best-known example of many types of Europe-Asia firm cooperation in technological development.

To improve on existing standards and reinforce the mesh of infrastructure links between Europe and Asia, it is also crucial to continue strengthening joint efforts in basic scientific research. Rightly, at a very early stage ASEM has declared its intentions to promote such links between various actors on an equal and voluntary basis, paying special attention to info-communications sectors. In its first report released in early 1999, the ASEM Vision Group suggested reinforcing science and technology contacts and recommended the establishment of an ASEM Information Technology Council that would include members from both the public and private sectors to promote information infrastructure development in such areas as technical standards, electronic translation software, and satellite TV broadcasting. A few months later, in October 1999, ASEM ministers of Science and Technology met for the first time in Beijing and noticed the many common interests ASEM members have. These include encouraging the creation of networks, promoting science and technology information and communication systems, establishing networks of centres of excellence in key technologies, and generally facilitating the mobility of scientists.

While the idea of an Asia-Europe Information Technology and Tele-communications programme or an Information Technology Council will probably only be fully clarified at the Seoul summit, whatever solution is reached should aim to avoid large conflicts of compatibility. To assure this, it could help link researchers with regional and national standardization bodies including the European Telecommunications Standardization Insti-tute in France, with the Standardisation activities of the Bangkok-based Asia-Pacific Telecommunity, always taking into account developments in other global, regional, and industry organizations.

INDUCING CONTENT CONNECTIONS

As the purpose of our ASEM travellers may be a combination of important business and some leisure, our ASEM bits likewise should be able to convey all types of quality content for any purpose and in all modes, including text, sounds and images. While Internet tools easily facilitate international commercial activity, there is still relatively little trade in educating content. While the Asia-Europe Foundation (ASEF) has so far shown remarkable leadership in linking ASEM countries through an array of cultural activities, occasionally using info-communications tools, ASEM travellers could develop more business and enjoy their travels much more if more virtual initiatives were implemented.

In its short life, ASEF has catalysed and facilitated value-added links by bringing together representatives from the media, as well as book publishers, museums and other cultural institutions in several gatherings. In the future, it could work with relevant info-communications institutions to develop virtual pilot projects that would promote truer images of ASEM partners and greater inter-regional sensitivities. The case of multilingual text communica-tions and processing is a good example of common ASEM concerns. After large US software firms tried to standardize language characters that would not allow non-English communications in the 1980s, many European and Asian countries collaborated to make sure that all the elements of their scripts, including all forms of Chinese ideograms, would be encoded alongside other non-English characters. Nowadays multilingualism is a feature of some software applications. But as some important types of multilingual communications tools, including email communications protocols, are still largely underdeveloped and fragmented, ASEM countries could collaborate at various levels of software to address those problems.

Another virtual activity could be the advancement in the automatic machine translation of words and documents. For administrative purposes the European Commission long used Systram, a document translation system for any pair of official languages used in European Union. In Asia, Japanese firms have been busily engaged in developing ways to translate whatever valuable information is available elsewhere into Japanese electronically. While other increasingly useful systems of uni- and bi-directional translation will soon emerge largely as the fruits of business initiatives, there is still a lot to do before fulfilling the ultimate goal of translating among most of the world's main languages, as being envisioned in a programme of the Tokyo campus of the United Nations University.

But text is just one aspect of multimedia applications. As ASEM members generally treasure the good to be derived from the past, while expecting to benefit from the best of new technologies which are rendering much easier than ever to generate, store, and share music, pictures and images, ASEM may promote common virtual cultural spaces. Bits should be freely downloaded at least by cultural and educational institutions so as to broaden access and appreciation of common human heritage.

How to integrate all those virtual spaces with cyberspace is a much bigger issue, as problems of software standardization grow when one gets closer to the level of human activity and culture. Even when infrastructures are connected, bits roam freely, and when end-users have figured out what information they are looking for, the desired information is often not available at any price because it has not yet been structured and catalogued. Furthermore, whatever has been linked to cyberspace often follows different criteria which means the results of the searches are rather limited. Thus, a key step in realizing a truly global, interactive, and multimedia knowledge library, will be to catalogue and make accessible existing contents found in libraries, archives, museums and other warehouses full of valuable data all over the world.

DREAMING ABOUT JOINING E-VISIONS

As our ASEM travellers increasingly hear music and watch images from so many cultures, new dreams may come into their heads. But then, with the turn of the millennium representing a point of no return for most of Europe and Asia in promoting information societies, and ASEM is still young and evolving, they should be bold and envision broad possibilities for profitable collaboration, as President Kim has been on his trip to Europe.

Largely following the leadership in info-communications developments of Nordic countries like Finland and Sweden, other European countries have by now started to implement plans to develop commerce, governments, and societies using new info-communications technologies, and increasingly within a regional perspective. In the European Summit that met in Helsinki in December 1999, the new president of the European Commission, Romano Prodi, presented an ambitious programme to promote Internet infrastructures, applications, and services throughout the EU early in the new century to connect every EU citizen to the Internet as quickly as possible and increase the growth of electronic commerce. This historic 'e-Europe' initiative will build on earlier efforts to liberalize and standarize domestic goods and services, and be reliant on science and technology co-operation. It would start by reducing the charge for local phone calls and Internet access through greater infrastructure liberalization, and would include the harmonization of frequencies for multimedia wireless by the end of 2001, the promotion of risk capital for hi-technology small businesses, and the development of smart cards for secure electronic access. To advance educational targets, all schools should soon have access to the Internet and multimedia resources, and all teachers should be skilled in the new technologies so as to achieve widespread digital literacy of pre-university students by the end of 2003. Other related initiatives should include the access to Internet services in public centres, the promotion of connections for disabled people, and on-line healthcare services.

Likewise, efforts among Asian ASEM members are picking up speed and showing some signs that may help create a more prosperous and stable regional community. In Southeast Asia, spurred by the competition created by the development of Singapore and Malaysia's Multimedia Super Corridor, other countries are working on their projects to top of their bent. And against the odds, the ASEAN process keeps developing on its way to becoming the most far-reaching regional co-operation process outside Europe. From a lessening distance, ASEAN is beginning to resemble the EU in many aspects, including its e-visions. As part of its far-reaching Vision 2020 goals, ASEAN also announced in late 1999 a far-reaching 'e-plan' for firms and states to develop its infrastructures and societies regionally aiming to achieve a great deal within the first decade of the new millennium. To achieve this purpose, the plan expects to establish a free trade area for goods, services, and investments in info-communications industries, increasing regional connectivity all the while. In the meantime, there continues to be progress in some important aspects like standardization of info-communications equipment.

In the past few years, in the wake of the 1997 financial crisis, ASEAN countries have also deepened their dialogue with Northeast Asia, where e-visions are also forward looking. Info-communications in Japan is experiencing a rapid change in an effort to catch-up and even leap-frog into the information age as Internet start-ups like those based in Shibuya's 'Bit Valley' are forcing a more rapid restructuring of traditional business conglomerates. And while Korea's rapid informatization often escapes the news, China's developments have not failed to attract global attention in 1999, the year in which its long-standing efforts to join the WTO included unprecedented commitments to open domestic telecommunications and Internet sectors to greater international competition. This would eventually only speed up China's overall efforts to convert state-owned enterprises into more efficient firms. Furthermore, the increasing number of Chinese alliances with entrepreneurial firms in Hong Kong, Taiwan and beyond prompt dreams of strengthening cyber-bamboo networks that would render territorial and developmental disputes obsolete.

STRENGHTENING ASEM AND INTERNET GOVERNANCE

Of course, as cyber-spaces have many global dimensions, any links between the visions of ASEM members will also have to take into account developments elsewhere. Within the broader Asian region, these include the standardization projects of the Bangkok-based Asia Pacific Telecommunity, the media exchanges promoted through the Kuala-Lumpur based Asia-Pacific Broadcasting Union, the Internet grassroots groups emerging from the Singapore-based Asia-Pacific Networking Group, the Tokyo-based Asian Info-communications Council, and even the Asia-Pacific Information Infrastructure developing within the broader APEC framework. At the truly global level, ASEM will also need to keep links with intergovernmental organizations like the International Telecommunications Union, the International Organisation for Standardisation, or the World Intellectual Property Organisation, as well as with other international consortia like the Internet Society and the World Wide Web, non-governmental institutions which are trying hard to adapt faster than ever to find relevant solutions to many Internet problems and enhance trust in the digital marketplace.

In the past decade efforts to bring some coherence to the globalization of trade and investment have largely been led by the WTO, exacting increased liberalization commitments to many types of info-communications goods and services through a combination of binding and non-binding agreements. While the credibility among its main members is surprisingly high, its global relevance and public trust can only increase once it takes into account the concerns of social actors and finally incorporates China. When this happens, president Kim's vision of contributing to an e-WTO round by linking the world through an e-network will be a step closer to coming true. In the meantime, ASEM should pay greater attention to ICANN, one of the latest additions to the global soup of key Internet acronyms. It stands for the Internet Corporation for Assigned Names and Numbers, a unique agency quickly established in 1998 in California under the auspices of the US Department of Commerce to give more shape to the global developments in electronic commerce including the famous '.com' top level domains. As it has become imperative to optimize the Internet Domain Name System so as to accommodate expected global growth and diversity, ICANN is charged with defining domain names, deciding which companies can sell them, as well as agreeing on policies to settle increasingly contentious trademark disputes over them.

Although ICANN's original group of directors was drawn mainly from Anglo-Saxon countries plus several Europeans and a Japanese, newer members give a better impression of the growth of electronic commerce in other parts of the world. Bearing this in mind, the ASEM process could take note of ICANN's development to make sure it continues to assure an effective global representation. Furthermore, it could consider reflecting on the consequences of developing an ASEM-related domain name policy, as it is possible that '.asem' could become a domain of interest at various levels. For instance, it is not beyond the bounds of imagination to think of ASEF's web-site being renamed www.asef.asem, or of Europe's political contribution to the overall ASEM process being accessible through www.asem.eu when the '.eu' regional top-level domain name is established, as it is likely to happen soon.

As many ASEM events have generated recondite web-page addresses, whoever performs the functions of a virtual ASEM secretariat would have as a priority the task of labelling them, as well as setting an open structure with external linkages to the many types of track II organizations concerned with ASEM, as well as with broader civil society initiatives. As a start, existing ASEM activities should clarify the scope of current addresses, like the unclear one of the ASEM Resource Centre web-site, announced in principle just to build on co-operative activities between the UK and the Philippines police through the provision of information to all those responsible for child welfare. Does this mean it will also promote education links, as the welfare of future generations basically depends on their access to sound education nowadays?

THE KEY IS EDUCATION

To realise the visions behind a more global and knowledge-based society more fully, we are all in need of a means to assess and manage the overflow of information and misinformation going through ever denser meshes of infrastructures with more insight and wisdom and of more widespread hardware equipment. As computing software alone will never be enough to achieve that goal, and global institutions are far from being effective, the key lies in a quick adaptation of education strategies aiming to develop globally-minded citizens who can learn continuously from childhood to their sunset years. And surprisingly, a virtual ASEM process may be in a unique position to go beyond the increasing *com.*mercialization of education and promote a life-long path to continuous knowledge upgrades.

ASEM has already taken some action in this direction and there are other virtual opportunities available. One far-reaching idea was Malaysia's project to create an Europe-Asia university, which has actually been launched by setting up a smaller-scale university centre in Kuala Lumpur. In the meantime, a series of networks are being developed or strengthened under the leadership of Singapore to promote ASEM education hubs. More recently, the ASEM Vision Group presented broad but bold proposals to enhance education and research exchanges, and other innovative projects including the use of new technologies, and even the creation of a virtual university. Those goals may now be more easily achieved as education systems everywhere are under strong pressure to speed up reforms.

Many countries in Europe are currently undergoing or seriously con-sidering important education changes to adapt to regional and global pressures and so as to be able to prepare human resources better for fuller employment in an innovation-based environment. As part of the e-Europe vision, the European Commission has launched an e-Learning initiative which strives to form public-private partnerships to equip schools as quickly as possible, train teachers, develop services and software, and speed up the networking of schools and teachers. It also expects to bring innovations in teaching methods and in individual learning styles so as to render learning an enjoyable activity for all. Aware of cultural pitfalls, it will take the diversity of cultures and systems into account. The catalyst of the vision will be the new phase of the European Commission's Socrates programme, which is basically committed to linking all countries in Western Europe, ASEM should explore extending those links to the many Asian countries that have made great efforts to develop their human resources and universities.

Japan, Korea, and Singapore are famous for having developed some of the most interesting models of pre-university education, and are now entering the race to upgrade their higher and continuing education systems, taking into account their international constraints and opportunities. Japan is also taking some global leadership in education issues upon itself as the new head of a more dynamic UNESCO is a Japanese diplomat, and as in April 2000 it hosted the first meeting ever of G8 ministers of education. Assiduously, Japan is making renewed efforts to attract Asian and other foreign students as part of its education 'big-bang' discussions. For their part, some ASEAN countries are increasing their number of higher education institutions, often by establishing novel types of electronically connected universities, and the group is steadily promoting a regional university network. Last but not at all least, China's newer plans to educate its large population include stronger international connections, as well as making full use of info-communications technologies.

Since info-communication tools will bring a major change to the world of universities, the opportunity is there to build beyond the idea of an ASEM on-line virtual university to catalyse virtual links among the many types of higher education institutions, which in turn should more easily build bridges to their communities as an increasing number of software-enabled tools are becoming available for that purpose. In Europe, the Commission is setting an openly accessible Internet gateway to the 'European Learning Area' with information on the full array of learning opportunities in Europe. That way, Asian countries could more easily learn about the affordable and high quality scientific and humanistic education in many European countries in their searches to find the right course or exchange opportunity. Conversely, Europeans should make a greater effort to profit from the opportunities in Asia, as high quality education is often affordable, and English is also increasingly being used there in many internationalization programmes.

The ASEM Vision Group proposed strengthening education links by establishing a high-profile scholarship scheme and visiting professorships. Actually, exchanges should be available at all levels between students, teaching and research staff, as well as administration, so as to achieve a critical mass that moves to modernize parochial national curricula as quickly as possible. To profit from globalization, young people should start early to learn the universality of basic science and technology as well as the basics of cultural diversities as seen, for instance, in human languages and artistic expressions. And using new info-communications technologies should not be a problem as youngsters keep proving they are the real masters behind the Internet revolutions. ASEM could then also help promote novel types of increasingly international, multi-cultural, and software-based life-long education, perhaps building from the ASEF December 1998 event that linked in real time Asian and European high schools. As Europe is also reinforcing the 'European Schoolnet' regional initiative to exchange information between schools, it could again carry this link a step further to reach Asian pre-university and vocational schools.

Finally, at the global level, ASEM might build upon the international efforts already undertaken by UNESCO to promote widespread education, at the OECD to define criteria for quality software, or by the Global Alliance on Transnational Education to certify and generally advocate quality cross-border education services in venues like the WTO. Only when many more people truly become globalized in their knowledge, will greater liberalization of international trade and investment be eagerly welcome in more places. ASEM intellectual growth will only then expand if intellectual property rights to monopolize the commercialization of information do not stop the construction of global virtual resource centres. Therefore, ASEM editors and academics could team up to build a dynamically expanding webliography linked to the increasing number of web-pages and web-sites generated by ASEM activities, the most relevant ones included in the table below. This in turn would create a virtual spiral of ASEM publications from an electronic community, in which different groups of people would contribute news, in-depth articles, and images to strengthen the weak links in the construction of a truly global virtual knowledge university.

MAIN ASEM-RELATED WEBSITES

Europe's overview of ASEM developments
http://europa.eu.int/comm/trade/bilateral/asem/asem.htm

ASEM 1 in 1996
http://asem.inter.net.th/

ASEM 2 in 1998
http://asem2.fco.gov.uk/

ASEM 3 in 2000
http://www.mofat.go.kr/asem3/eng/e_main.html

Asia-Europe Vision Group
http://www.mofat.go.kr/aevg

Asia-Europe Foundation
http://www.asef.org

2nd Asia-Europe Young Leaders' Symposium in 1998
http://www.aeyls-ii.bka.gv.at/

3rd Asia-Europe Young Leaders' Symposium in 1999
http://www.mofat.go.kr/aeylsiii/

ASEM Trust Fund
http://europa.eu.int/comm/dg15/efex/

Investment Promotion Action Plan
http://www.asem.vie.net

ASEMConnect
http://www.asemconnect.com.sg/

ASEM Ministerial Conference on Science & Technology
http://www.cordis.lu/asem

ASEM Resource Centre - Child Welfare Initiative
http://www.asem.org

PART FIVE
ANNEXES

ANNEX 1

CHAIRMAN'S STATEMENT ASEM 3

INTRODUCTION

1. The Third Asia-Europe Meeting (ASEM 3) was held in Seoul on 20-21 October 2000. It was attended by Heads of State and Government from ten Asian and fifteen European nations, with the President of the French Republic acting also as President of the Council of the European Union, and the President of the European Commission. Leaders were accompanied by their Foreign Ministers, a member of the European Commission and other Ministers. This momentous Meeting was chaired by the President of the Republic of Korea.

2. Leaders recalled the inaugural Summit in Bangkok on 1-2 March 1996 (ASEM 1), which forged a new comprehensive Asia-Europe Partnership for Greater Growth, envisaging co-operation between Asia and Europe in the political, economic, cultural and other areas, and the second Summit in London on 3-4 April 1998 (ASEM 2), where Leaders reinforced this partnership notably through their commitment to working together to address the economic and financial crisis in Asia.

Leaders recognized the Third ASEM in Seoul as a historic milestone in the evolution of the ASEM process, which provided a unique opportunity both to review achievements to date and to set the broad direction to take ASEM forward into a new millennium. Leaders reaffirmed their commitment to strengthening the Asia-Europe partnership and confirmed their intention to meet again at ASEM 4 in Copenhagen in 2002.

3. Leaders noted with satisfaction the progress made in the ASEM process since the Second ASEM on the basis of the principles agreed at the Bangkok and London Summits and set out in the Asia-Europe Co-operation Framework (AECF). They appreciated the discussions at the second Foreign, Economic and Finance Ministers' Meetings in 1999 and welcomed the holding of the Science and Technology Ministers' Meeting also in 1999.

DEVELOPMENTS IN THE TWO REGIONS

4. Leaders noted with particular satisfaction the clear signs of recovery in the Asian countries affected by the financial and economic crisis and recognized the importance of continued reform in the light of specific situations in countries concerned. They acknowledged that ASEM had played a crucial role in bringing Asia and Europe together to work in conjunction to address this crisis. They expressed their confidence that the renewed economic dynamism of Asia and the growing economic strength of Europe would in synergy promote prosperity and stability in both regions, thereby benefiting the international community as a whole in this increasingly interdependent world.

In this regard, expressing concern over volatility in oil prices, Leaders shared the view that ensuring a stable supply of energy, including oil and other fuels, was vital to the maintenance of long-term economic growth for all ASEM partners and the world at large.

5. Leaders welcomed the admission of Cambodia as a new member of ASEAN at the Special ASEAN Foreign Ministers' Meeting in Hanoi in April 1999 ("ASEAN 10") and noted ASEAN's achievement of their goal of embracing all the ten countries in Southeast Asia. They also acknowledged that great progress had been made in East Asian co-operation at the ASEAN + 3 Summit held in Manila in November 1999, where ASEAN countries, China, Japan and the Republic of Korea affirmed the importance of meeting on a regular basis and adopted the Joint Statement on East Asia Co-operation. In this connection, they welcomed the progress made at the inaugural ASEAN+3 Foreign Ministers' Meeting held in Bangkok in July 2000. They further welcomed the progress made at the ASEAN+3 Finance Ministers' Meeting held in Chiang Mai in May 2000 and the ASEAN+3 Economic Ministers' Meeting also held in Chiang Mai in October 2000, as further strengthening East Asian financial and economic co-operation.

Leaders also took note of the continued development of the ASEAN Regional Forum (ARF) as an important forum for dialogue and co-operation on regional, political and security issues and welcomed the admission of the Democratic People's Republic of Korea (DPRK) in July 2000 as a significant step which has further strengthened the ARF and would help contribute to advancing the cause of regional peace and security.

6. Leaders welcomed the introduction of the euro and noted that it will contribute to greater exchange rate stability in the international monetary

system. They also noted progress in the European Union Intergovernmental Conference to strengthen institutions of the European Union as well as in the European Union enlargement process. They further noted developments in security co-operation within the context of the Common Foreign and Security Policy, such as the European Security and Defence Policy.

FOSTERING POLITICAL DIALOGUE

7. Leaders noted that on the basis of the guiding principles for conducting political dialogue as established at the Bangkok and London Summits, the first and second ASEM Foreign Ministers' Meetings, and the regular Senior Officials' Meetings had been the occasion for useful discussions of regional and global issues of common concern, and had contributed to enhancing mutual awareness and understanding between partners.

8. Leaders reaffirmed their commitment to pursuing a secure international environment for all countries and to intensifying co-operation between Asia and Europe with a view to contributing towards international peace, stability and prosperity, and respect for international law. From this standpoint, they engaged in detailed discussions on regional and international issues of common interest.

Leaders welcomed the historic first inter-Korean Summit held in June 2000 in Pyongyang and acknowledged the great significance of this event which has laid the foundation for the peace process on the Korean peninsula. In recognition of the importance of this process, a separate declaration has been issued on the recent developments on the Korean peninsula.

Leaders welcomed the progress toward the restoration of stability in East Timor and encouraged further efforts by UNTAET, in co-operation with the countries closely involved, in order to guarantee the success of the transition process. They shared the view that the rehabilitation and nation building process in East Timor should be actively and continuously supported by the international community as a whole.

They also recognized the important steps taken and the urgency to solve the problems still remaining, concerning the East Timorese refugees in West Timor, in a comprehensive manner. These actions should be aimed at ensuring reconciliation, peace and harmony for all Timorese.

Leaders stressed the importance of developing co-operation between the states of Southeastern Europe and in this context welcomed the Stability

Pact and noted its aims. They also underlined the importance of the full implementation of UN Security Council Resolution 1244 in Kosovo.

Leaders expressed their concern at the situation in the Middle East. They welcomed the Summit in Sharm El Sheikh, which reached an agreement on measures in order to put an end to violence. They called upon the parties to put those measures into effect without delay.

Leaders welcomed the successful conclusion of the Millennium Summit held on 6-8 September this year at the headquarters of the United Nations. They particularly welcomed world leaders' renewed commitment to the purposes and principles of the United Nations Charter and reaffirmed the key objectives of the international community in the 21st century as identified in the Millennium Declaration. In this context, Leaders expressed their commitment to UN reform, with the goal of strengthening and enhancing the representativeness, transparency, and effectiveness of the UN system, including the Security Council. They also called for better co-ordination between the UN and other relevant organizations in the area of development co-operation and confirmed the importance of sounder UN finances as well as providing the UN with sufficient financial resources to enable it to fulfill its mandate.

Leaders committed themselves to promote and protect all human rights, including the right to development, and fundamental freedoms, bearing in mind their universal, indivisible and interdependent character as expressed at the World Conference on Human Rights in Vienna.

Expressing their grave concern over the recurrent armed conflicts around the world, Leaders agreed to work together for effective prevention of conflicts in conformity with the UN Charter and international law. They also underlined the importance of maintaining global strategic balance and stability, and strengthening regional and global initiatives on arms control, disarmament, and non-proliferation of weapons of mass-destruction. They further expressed their determination to preserve the integrity and validity of existing international arms control and disarmament treaties and to further develop ASEM dialogue and co-operation in these fields. They welcomed the successful results of the Treaty on the Non-Proliferation of Nuclear Weapons (NPT) Review Conference and looked forward to the full implementation of the Final Document adopted by consensus at the Conference. They reaffirmed their support for: the early entry into force of the Comprehensive Nuclear-Test-Ban Treaty; an immediate commencement of the negotiations in the Conference on Disarmament on a Fissile Material

Cut-off Treaty, within the framework of an agreed working programme, with a view to their conclusion within five years; and an early conclusion of Ad Hoc Group negotiations on measures to strengthen the Biological and Toxin Weapons Convention. They further noted the progress made by the Organization for the Prohibition of Chemical Weapons in implementing the Chemical Weapons Convention and stressed the need to actively promote universality. Leaders appreciated the international community's efforts to deal with the suffering and casualties caused by indiscriminate use of anti-personnel land mines (APL) and support international assistance for training in demining, the removal of unexploded ordnance and the rehabilitation of victims. They also stressed the need to address the issue of small arms and light weapons, and agreed to work together for the success of the UN Conference on the Illicit Trade in Small Arms and Light Weapons in All Its Aspects in 2001.

Leaders shared the view that a rapidly changing world represents formidable challenges to the whole international community. In this regard, they expressed their commitment to ASEM playing a constructive role in pro-moting increased multilateral dialogue and co-operation, based on equal partnership, mutual respect and mutual benefit, and in building a new international political and economic order in light of the growing interdependence of Asia and Europe and the changing international environment.

9. Building on the conclusions of the Bangkok and London Summits and the Asia-Europe Co-operation Framework 2000, Leaders expressed their commitment to addressing global issues of common concern such as managing migratory flows in a globalized world and transnational crime, including money laundering; smuggling and exploitation of migrants and trafficking in persons, in particular of women and children for the purpose of sexual exploitation; international terrorism and piracy; racism and xenophobia; the fight against illegal drugs; the welfare of women and children; community health care improvement; the fight against HIV/AIDS, infectious and parasitic diseases; as well as food security and supply. In this respect, Leaders expressed their firm support for the adoption of the UN Convention against Transnational Organized Crime and its protocols by the end of the year 2000.

Leaders acknowledged that the degradation of the natural resource base and, in particular, the problem of energy and environment, is a challenge for all ASEM partners and reiterated their commitment to addressing global environmental issues, to ensuring a successful Sixth Conference of the

Parties to the UN Framework Convention on Climate Change in November 2000, and to working towards the early entry into force of the Kyoto Protocol. In this context, they underscored the great importance of environmental protection and enhanced co-operation among ASEM partners. In this connection, they noted with appreciation the progress made by the Asia-Europe Environmental Technology Centre (AEETC) in Thailand since its formal opening in March 1999 and supported its efforts to act as a catalyst for enhanced co-operation in the environmental field.

REINFORCING CO-OPERATION IN THE ECONOMIC AND FINANCIAL FIELDS

10. Leaders committed themselves to promoting greater economic linkages between ASEM partners as an indispensable element of a strong partnership between the two regions. They noted in particular the substantial contribution of the trade and investment pledge made at ASEM 2 in stabilizing the economies hit by the Asian crisis and providing a strong basis for renewed growth in the region. They also welcomed the results of the second Economic Ministers' Meeting held in Berlin in October 1999 and those of the Senior Officials' Meetings on Trade and Investment.

Leaders decided to further intensify their efforts to increase trade and investment flows between the two regions and expressed satisfaction with the progress made in relation to the Trade Facilitation Action Plan (TFAP), particularly the concrete goals achieved since ASEM 2 as reflected in the report of the overall evaluation of TFAP, the addition of e-commerce as a new priority area, and the agreement to prepare voluntary annual reports on the status of individual partners to overcome the major generic barriers to trade as identified collectively by ASEM partners. They also noted the positive steps taken by SOMTI in implementing the Investment Promotion Action Plan (IPAP) including the expansion of the Virtual Information Exchange (VIE) website, which provides, *inter alia*, information on the investment regimes and opportunities of partners, and the compilation of a list of most effective measures to promote foreign direct investment (FDI), which was endorsed by Economic Ministers as a non-binding benchmark for partners. They asked Economic Ministers to maintain the momentum to ensure that these, and other mechanisms to be developed, will be implemented effectively to strengthen trade and investment regimes between Asia and Europe in an open and transparent manner. To this end, they endorsed the work programme annexed to the Trade Facilitation Action Plan: TFAP Deliverables and Goals for 2000-2002.

In this age of knowledge, information, and globalization, Leaders recognized the importance of co-operation in the areas of information and communications technology as well as trade and investment. Leaders shared the view that information and communications technology have become pivotal engines of growth in the world economy and also that the resulting digital divide would deepen economic and social disparities in and among countries. With this in mind, they agreed to accelerate efforts to address the digital divide to promote the joint prosperity of the two regions and instructed Economic Ministers to review the progress made in this area. In this context, they also emphasized the need to establish and expand information and research networks between the two regions and among ASEM partners in order to facilitate the flow of knowledge and information as well as research exchanges.

11. Leaders reiterated the importance of a rules-based multilateral trading system in promoting global growth, prosperity and sustainable development and meeting the challenges of globalization. In this regard, they underlined their commitment to work together to promote further liberalization and to strengthen and develop rules through a new round of multilateral trade negotiations. They agreed to intensify their efforts with other WTO Members to launch such a round at the earliest opportunity. The negotiating agenda should reflect an overall balance, which responds to the interests of all WTO Members, including developing country Members. This would more likely be achieved by an inclusive approach to the agenda setting, with no a priori exclusion of subjects of interest to individual WTO Members, seeking to secure the WTO's continued relevance in the globalized world economy. To this end, they stressed that strong political will and greater flexibility as well as open and constructive dialogue among all WTO members would be necessary to lay the ground for the necessary consensus decision on the launching of a round.

Leaders welcomed the positive and constructive manner in which the negotiations under the built-in agenda have so far been carried out and pledged to actively pursue these negotiations in good faith. They recognized that more meaningful and balanced results within a reasonable time frame could be achieved if negotiations were conducted as part of a new round. In this regard, there was also a general understanding among them that further progress in the mandated negotiations would in turn have a positive effect on such multilateral negotiations.
Leaders also stressed that the interests and concerns of developing and least-developed countries should be duly addressed through various means, including, *inter alia*, improved market access opportunities and technical

assistance for enhanced capacity-building, and addressing issues related to the implementation of Uruguay Round undertakings.

Leaders recognized that full participation in the WTO by ASEM partners will strengthen the system and reaffirmed their support for the acceleration of current accession negotiations of ASEM non-WTO Members, through the exchange of information, experience and technical co-operation, that would be based on mutually acceptable market access commitments and adherence to WTO rules. Leaders also stressed the importance of sustaining broad public support for the multilateral trading system and agreed to strengthen efforts to improve their engagement with the public regarding the benefits and challenges of trade liberalization. Noting that the number of regional trade arrangements has been increasing in recent years, Leaders stressed the primacy of a multilateral trading system. In this regard, they agreed to ensure that all regional trade arrangements are consistent with WTO rules, complementing the multilateral trading system.

12. Noting with satisfaction that with substantial support from the international community, Asia is well on the way to recovery from the economic and financial crisis which broke out in 1997, Leaders assessed the status of ASEM activities aimed at strengthening co-operation in the financial area, particularly in preventing the recurrence of a crisis.

In this context, they reviewed the results of the second Finance Ministers' Meeting held in Frankfurt/Main in January 1999 and thereby recognized the significant impact of specific initiatives such as the ASEM Trust Fund and the European Financial Expertise Network in addressing problems in the financial and social sectors. They welcomed the progress made in the implementation of sound financial regulation, in particular in the Basel Core Principles for effective banking supervision. They also welcomed the steps already taken to strengthen the international financial architecture. Leaders recalled the crucial role of reform in creating the conditions for sound long-term growth, and invited European and Asian partners to exchange experiences on their respective economic reform efforts.

Leaders welcomed the achievements of the ASEM Trust Fund (ATF) in helping alleviate the impact of the economic and financial crisis on affected Asian countries. They supported the extension of the ATF into a Phase 2. In this connection, they called on the Finance Ministers in their Meeting in Kobe in January 2001 to determine the modalities for a Phase 2 ATF.

Upon assessing the vulnerability of the international financial market, Leaders agreed to take further measures to strengthen the international financial system and ensure long-term stability, stressing the importance of domestic financial reform and corporate governance. They agreed to make every effort to put the principle of orderly financial liberalization into practice. Leaders emphasized the need to implement codes and standards. They took note of the Financial Stability Forum's work on Highly Leveraged Institutions, and stressed the importance of implementing indirect regulations. They stressed that direct regulation would be considered if, upon review, the implementation of indirect regulation was not adequately addressing the concerns identified. They also reaffirmed that they remained committed to addressing potential problems associated with international volatile capital movement. In addition, they reiterated the need to enhance regulation in problematic Offshore Financial Centres, and underlined from this perspective the crucial role that the fight against money laundering should play in strengthening market integrity and therefore financial stability as a whole. In this perspective, they strongly supported the Financial Action Task Force's recommendations and their inclusion among the priority international standards. They also stressed the necessity of systematically involving private creditors in crisis prevention and resolution. They recognized the role of regional economic and monetary co-operation in promoting international stability, as exemplified by EMU.

Leaders encouraged the upcoming Finance Ministers' Meeting to study how European partners could share their experiences with Asian partners in fostering regional economic and monetary co-operation. They also asked Finance Ministers to examine how Asian partners could take into account major changes in the international monetary system resulting from the introduction of the euro.

Leaders expressed strong expectations that the third ASEM Finance Ministers' Meeting in Kobe would make further substantial developments in monetary and financial matters.

13. Leaders reiterated the need for ASEM to promote dialogue and co-operation between the business communities of the two regions and emphasized the central role of the Asia-Europe Business Forum (AEBF), reinforced with the adoption of the AEBF Guidelines in 1999. Leaders welcomed the positive results and the input from the AEBF concerning *inter alia*, trade facilitation and investment promotion as evidence of deepening business sector engagement in the ASEM process. They invited the AEBF to play a more active role in the activities carried out to implement TFAP and IPAP. Recognizing that SMEs comprise the core economic activity of all countries and are essential in creating new jobs, Leaders welcomed the results of the

Asia-Europe SME Conference and Seminar, and efforts on the part of the AEBF in encouraging Asian and European SMEs to pursue growth and prosperity in tandem and the development of networks among SME organizations to promote and facilitate SME activities between the two regions. They also welcomed the setting up of ASEM Connect to facilitate on-line business matching and access to information as part of ASEM's efforts to address the needs of SMEs.

14. Leaders, emphasizing the importance of Science and Technology (S&T), welcomed the results of the ASEM Science and Technology Ministers' Meeting (STMM) held in Beijing in October 1999. They welcomed the concrete progress since this meeting in measures to enhance S&T co-operation between Asia and Europe. They called for an intensification and further follow-up activities in areas of common interest and priorities identified at the meeting. These range from issues calling for global solutions, such as biodiversity conservation, bio-safety, including food security and sustainable economic and social development, etc. to the upgrading of research capacities of enterprises, the development of e-commerce and information technology, knowledge transfer from research institutes/universities to industry, S&T human resource development and agricultural S&T issues. Co-operation in these areas will be enhanced through the promotion of joint research, the exchange of researchers, seminars, training courses and networks of centres of excellence.

PROMOTING CO-OPERATION IN OTHER AREAS, INCLUDING SOCIAL AND CULTURAL ISSUES

15. Leaders underscored the importance of enhancing mutual understanding between the two regions through closer people-to-people exchanges of various kinds in the social and cultural areas. Leaders also recognized the vivid and diverse cultures of Asia and Europe as a source of vitality to enliven the mutual co-operation between the two regions and noted that ASEM is an excellent vehicle to achieve this end.

Leaders recognized the crucial importance of education and agreed that a key priority should be to enhance the contacts and exchanges in this field, including student and academic exchanges, interuniversity co-operation and the facilitation of electronic networking between schools in the two regions. In this regard, they undertook to explore the possibility of mutual recognition of degrees, licences, etc., between educational institutions of the two regions. They also recognized the potential for the ASEM Education

Hubs (AEH) and the Asia-Europe University (AEU) and other related activities in expanding educational co-operation, promoting greater cross-cultural contacts and fostering mutual understanding between Asia and Europe.

16. Agreeing on the need to ensure that the benefits of globalization are widely shared while reducing its adverse effects, Leaders expressed their commitment to strengthening the dialogue on socio-economic issues among partners. They underlined the importance of social and human resource development, including life-long learning, for the alleviation of economic and social disparities within and among ASEM countries, as well as for the sustained growth of both Asia and Europe and for promoting sustainable development in less developed areas such as the Mekong Subregion. They also confirmed their intention to enhance social safety nets to promote the welfare of the socially vulnerable. Leaders welcomed the outcome of the 24th Special Session of the United Nations General Assembly on the Implementation of the Outcome of the World Summit for Social Development, held on 26-30 June 2000 in Geneva, to review progress in the implementation of the Copenhagen Declaration of 1995. They expressed their commitment to overcome impediments to social development by adhering to the principles and goals of the Copenhagen+5 and by implementing the further actions and initiatives identified in the special session.

17. Leaders recognized the important role played by ASEF in promoting people-to-people contact, intellectual linkages and cultural exchanges between Asia and Europe since its establishment in February 1997, and reaffirmed their full support for ASEF's role as a key vehicle in increasing mutual understanding between the two regions. Leaders also took this opportunity to thank the outgoing management team of ASEF for their achievements and to welcome the new management team.

TAKING FORWARD THE ASEM PROCESS

18. Building on the conclusions of the Bangkok and London Summits, Leaders:
- welcomed the Asia-Europe Vision Group Report submitted to ASEM 3. They expressed their appreciation to the members of the Group for their efforts in producing this Report which sets out a medium to long-term vision for the ASEM process and numerous valuable recommendations for promoting mutual co-operation between Asia and Europe;

- adopted the Asia-Europe Co-operation Framework 2000 (AECF 2000), drawn up on the basis of the AECF approved by the Leaders at ASEM 2 in London, and setting out the vision, principles and objectives, priorities and mechanisms for the ASEM process for the first decade of the 21st century.

19. In addition to the co-operation identified at the Bangkok and London Summits, and with a view to advancing the objectives and priorities set out in the Asia-Europe Co-operation Framework 2000, now adopted.

Leaders:

endorsed the following new ASEM initiatives:

Globalization/Information Technology
   Conference on E-commerce and Logistics
   Initiative to Address the Digital Divide
   Roundtable on Globalization
   Seminar on Asia-Europe Co-operation in SMEs
   Seminar on Information and Telecommunications Technology
   Trans-Eurasia Information Network
   WTO Trade Facilitation Conference (Transnational and Law Enforce-ment-related Matters)
   Anti-corruption Initiative
   Anti-money Laundering Initiative
   Initiative to Combat Trafficking in Women and Children
   Symposium on Law Enforcement Organs' Co-operation in Combating Transnational Crimes

Human Resources Development/Environment/Health
   DUO, Fellowship Programme
   Environment Ministers' Meeting
   Initiative on HIV/AIDS
   Ministerial Conference on Co-operation for the Management of Migratory Flows Europe-Asia
   Science and Technology Co-operation on Forestry Conservation and Sustainable Development

- and took note of the following new activities proposed to ASEM and encouraged their further development within the context of the Asia-Europe Co-operation Framework 2000:

Collaborative Research Program on Networking
Human Resource Development in Information and Communications Technology
Lifelong Learning
Overcoming Cultural Nuances: Toward a New Public Management
Project for a Euro-Asian Network for the Monitoring and Control of Communicable Diseases
Promoting Business Opportunities in ASEM
Seminar on Asia-Europe Co-operation on the Applications of Information Technology to Human Resources Development in the Mekong Sub-region

20. Looking forward to meeting at ASEM 4 in Copenhagen, Denmark in 2002, Leaders decided to hold the Fifth ASEM in Asia in 2004. They noted that, for the year 2001, Foreign, Economic and Finance Ministers would meet in China, Vietnam and Japan respectively. Leaders instructed Ministers to make a decision on the specific date and venue of their respective meetings for the year 2002 before ASEM 4.

Seoul 21 October 2000

ANNEX 2

ASIA-EUROPE CO-OPERATION FRAMEWORK 2000

I. INTRODUCTION

1. At the inaugural Asia-Europe Meeting (ASEM) in Bangkok on 1-2 March 1996, all participants agreed to work together to create a new Asia-Europe partnership, to build a greater understanding between the people of the two regions, and to establish a strengthened dialogue among equals.

2. The second ASEM in London on 3-4 April 1998 confirmed the important role which ASEM has played, and will continue to play, in reinforcing the partnership between Asia and Europe in the political, economic, cultural and other areas of co-operation. That Meeting also adopted an Asia-Europe Co-operation Framework (AECF) to guide, focus and co-ordinate ASEM activities, and commissioned an Asia-Europe Vision Group to develop a medium to long-term vision to help guide the ASEM process into the 21st century.

3. The third ASEM in Seoul on 20-21 October 2000 was a historic milestone in the evolution of the ASEM process and provided an opportunity to review progress and achievements so far and to consolidate this foundation for a comprehensive and sustained co-operation between the two regions

4. The AECF adopted by Heads of State/Government at ASEM 3 in Seoul in 2000 sets out the vision, principles, objectives, priorities and mechanisms for the ASEM process for the first decade of the new millennium.

II. A VISION INTO THE 21ST CENTURY

5. Recognising that the Asia-Europe Meeting was initiated with the aim of strengthening links between Asia and Europe in this era of growing global interdependence, ASEM partners have agreed to strive for a common goal of maintaining and enhancing peace and stability as well as promoting conditions conducive to sustainable economic and social development. ASEM Leaders envisage Asia and Europe as an area of peace and shared development with common interests and aspirations such as upholding the purposes and principles of the UN Charter, respect for democracy, the rule

of law, equality, justice and human rights, concern for the environment and other global issues, eradication of poverty, protection of cultural heritage and the promotion of intellectual endeavours, economic and social development, knowledge and educational resources, science and technology, commerce, investment and enterprise. To this end, Asia and Europe, building a comprehensive and future-oriented partnership, should work together to address challenges and to translate them into common opportunities. They should in particular be addressed through our dialogue and joint endeavours in relation to political, economic, and social, cultural and educational issues. ASEM partners also recognise the need to work together in addressing the new challenges posed by, among other things, globalisation, information technology, e-commerce and the New Economy.

6. Synergy between Asia and Europe will be of tremendous value, not only for the two regions but also for the global community as a whole. Strengthened dialogue and co-operation between Asia and Europe in a spirit of equal partnership and mutual benefit will also enhance international co-operation, thereby contributing positively to security, prosperity and sustainable development for the benefit of all and to building a new international political and economic order, taking into account changes in the international arena including globalization.

III. KEY PRINCIPLES AND OBJECTIVES

7. The first ASEM in Bangkok agreed to develop a common vision of the future, to foster political dialogue, to reinforce economic co-operation, and to promote co-operation in other areas.

8. The second ASEM in London reaffirmed the key role which the partnership between Asia and Europe should play in a highly-interdependent world, and pursued our work in fostering political dialogue, reinforcing economic co-operation, and promoting co-operation in other areas, including social, cultural and global issues. The Summit confirmed that the ASEM process should:

> be conducted on a basis of equal partnership, mutual respect and mutual benefit;
> be an open and evolutionary process: enlargement should be conducted on the basis of consensus by the Heads of State/Government;

enhance mutual understanding and awareness through a process of
dialogue and lead to co-operation on the identification of priorities for
concerted and supportive action;

carry forward the three key dimensions with the same impetus: fostering
political dialogue, reinforcing economic co-operation, and promoting co-
operation in other areas;

as an informal process, ASEM need not be institutionalised. It should
stimulate and facilitate progress in other forums;

go beyond governments in order to promote dialogue and co-operation
between the business/private sectors of the two regions and, no less
importantly, between the peoples of the two regions.

ASEM should also encourage the co-operative activities of think tanks and
research groups of both regions.

9. Reflecting the common desire to strengthen the political dialogue between
Asia and Europe, this should be fostered by highlighting and expanding
common ground, by enhancing understanding and friendship, and by
promoting and deepening co-operation. As agreed at the Bangkok and
London Summits, this comprehensive political dialogue should be
conducted on the basis of the principles reflected in paragraphs 5,6 and 7 of
the Bangkok Chair Statement.

10. Acknowledging that the growing economic links between the two
regions formed the basis for a strong partnership, the Bangkok Summit had
agreed to forge a new comprehensive Asia-Europe Partnership for Greater
Growth. Events since then have amply confirmed the importance of this
partnership in a highly-interdependent global economy, as emphasised at the
London Summit.

11 In promoting co-operation in other areas, the Bangkok and London
Summits had likewise affirmed the importance to be attached to co-
operation in the cultural and social fields, responding to and encouraging the
wide interest in strengthening links between the two regions shown by the
public, think-tanks, research groups, universities and all sectors of society
generally, thereby promoting the human dimension in the ASEM process.
Building on the discussions in Bangkok, the London Summit had also
reiterated the importance to be attached to enhancing the ASEM dialogue on
global issues.

IV. KEY PRIORITIES

12. In the political field, ASEM efforts should focus on issues of common interest, proceeding step-by-step in a process of consensus-building, with a view to enhancing mutual awareness and understanding between partners, drawing strength from our diversity while not excluding any issue beforehand but exercising wisdom and judiciousness in selecting the topics for discussion. The political dialogue should be conducted on the basis of mutual respect, equality, promotion of fundamental rights and, in accordance with the rules of international law and obligations, non-intervention, whether direct or indirect, in each other's internal affairs.

13. In this context, key priorities shall include:
   intensifying the high-level political dialogue, including at SOM level;
   taking forward the dialogue on issues of common interest arising in the context of relevant international institutions, including on UN reform;
   enhancing our informal political dialogue on regional and international issues of common interest, in line with the principles laid down in Bangkok and London and confirmed in this present AECF, including informal ASEM seminars and workshops, proposed by individual partners and endorsed by SOM, in the fields of international relations, politics and economics.

14. ASEM efforts should also address global issues of common concern such as:
   strengthening efforts in the global and regional context towards arms control, disarmament and non-proliferation of weapons of mass destruction;
   combating illicit trafficking in and accumulation of small arms and light weapons; ¡¤ promoting the welfare of women and children;
   enhancing the ASEM dialogue and co-operation on other global issues such as human resources development, community health care improvement, and food security and supply;
   tackling the global environmental issues, striving for sustainable development, and supporting the work of the Asia-Europe Environmental Technology Centre;
   managing migratory flows in a globalized world;
   combating transnational crime, including money laundering, the smuggling and exploitation of migrants, the trafficking of persons in particular women and children, international terrorism and piracy, and fighting against illegal drugs;
   combating racism and xenophobia.

15. In the economic and financial fields, ASEM efforts should focus on strengthening dialogue and co-operation between the two regions, with a view to facilitating sustainable economic growth, contributing together to the global economic dialogue and addressing the impact of globalisation.

16. In this context, key priorities shall include:

intensifying dialogue in Economic Ministers' Meeting and Senior Officials' Meeting on Trade and Investment (SOMTI), with particular regard to:

- complementing and reinforcing efforts to strengthen the open and rules-based multilateral trading system embodied in the WTO. Full participation in the WTO by ASEM partners will strengthen the organization;
- strengthening two-way trade and investment flows between Asia and Europe, notably through the active implementation and further enhancement of the Trade Facilitation and Investment Promotion Action Plans (TFAP and IPAP);
- establishing an enhanced climate for business-to-business dialogue and co-operation between the two regions, emphasising the central role of the Asia-Europe Business Forum (AEBF) and the importance of continuity therein, facilitating two-way dialogue between government and the business/private sector in order to respond to the concrete issues facing our business community, and paying particular attention to the problems faced by SMEs;
- enhancing dialogue and co-operation in priority industrial sectors, focusing on high technology sectors of common interest, for example, agro-technology, food processing, bio-technology, information and telecommunication (including e-commerce), transport, energy, environmental engineering, etc.;

Intensifying dialogue in Finance Ministers' Meeting and Finance Deputies' Meeting with particular regard to:

- enhancing our dialogue on global financial issues, including the international financial architecture;
- enhancing co-operation, *inter alia* on technical assistance, the exchange of expertise, and the monitoring of trends, in relation to the prevention of possible future crises;
- enhancing macro-economic policy consultation;
- strengthening co-operation in financial supervision and regulation;
- strengthening co-operation against money-laundering;
- strengthening customs co-operation;

enhancing our dialogue in the field of science and technology, promoting networking and exchanges among researchers and policy-makers, particularly in priority fields of common interest;

enhancing a broad-based dialogue on key issues relating to the sustained development of our two regions and of the global economy including important socio-economic issues.

17. In the social, cultural and educational fields, ASEM efforts should focus on promoting enhanced contact and strengthened mutual awareness between the people of our two regions, with a view to helping peoples in Europe and Asia to be more aware of the common issues affecting our common future, and to better understand each other through dialogue.

18. In this context, ASEM partners should continue strong support and encouragement for ASEF which is an important vehicle to promote and catalyse cultural, intellectual and people-to-people exchanges.

19. In this same context, key priorities shall include:

enhancing our contacts and exchanges in the field of education, including student, academic and information exchanges, inter-university co-operation, facilitating electronic networking between schools, exploring the possibilities for mutual recognition of degrees and licenses between our educational and related institutions, and substantially increasing student exchanges between our two regions, reflecting work being carried forward through, *inter alia*, the ASEM Education Hubs, the Asia-Europe University and other initiatives;

strengthening our dialogue and co-operation in the protection and promotion of cultural heritage;

promoting networking and sharing of experience in the social sciences, arts, humanities and sports;

encouraging a broad-based dialogue and networking among all sectors of society, including *inter alia* parliamentary representatives;

improving dissemination of information about ASEM in the public and about the importance of closer Asia-Europe relations.

20. These priorities will be updated by Heads of State and Government at their Summit meetings. They will form the basis of two-year work programmes drawn up by Foreign Ministers on the occasion of each Summit, and reviewed and updated at the Foreign Ministers' meetings between Summits.

V. MECHANISMS FOR CO-ORDINATING, FOCUSING AND MANAGING ASEM ACTIVITIES

21. Foreign Ministers, Economic Ministers and Finance Ministers will meet on a regular basis, normally once a year. Occasional conferences bringing together other Ministers may be decided upon by Heads of State/Government as appropriate.

22. As established by the Bangkok Summit and confirmed in London, Foreign Ministers and Senior Officials (SOM) are responsible for the overall co-ordination of ASEM activities. ASEM Co-ordinators, to be appointed by their respective regions, shall facilitate the co-ordination of the ASEM process.

23. To facilitate a rapid and effective exchange of information among all ASEM partners and their relevant officials, the network of ASEM contact officers, appointed by Foreign Ministers, will provide a direct and informal channel of communications.

24. Economic Ministers (including SOMTI) and Finance Ministers (including their deputies) should be the primary channels for carrying forward the ASEM work programme in their respective areas. They would each provide their inputs to the work programme to be co-ordinated and put together by the SOM and Foreign Ministers. Their respective senior officials will liaise closely with the SOM through a regular exchange of information. Officials from the co-ordinating partners will assist in this co-ordination and liaison.

25. To be included in the ASEM work programme, any proposed ASEM initiative should have the support of all ASEM partners, and should be in line with the principles, objectives and priorities set out in this AECF. In addition, any proposed ASEM initiative should meet the following guidelines:
   the proposed initiative should be of mutual benefit, and must receive the full consensus of all ASEM partners;
   it should contribute to advance the overall objectives and perspectives of the ASEM process; ¡¤ the participation of a large number of ASEM partners must be ensured;
   the proposal should clearly state goals, prime actors (government, business, civil society), target audience, likely cost, and possible means of finance;
   duplication with existing ASEM initiatives should be avoided;

initiatives should, where suitable, have a counterpart Asian and European partner;

participation will be open to ASEM partners only, though SOM may, on a case-by-case basis and with the consensus of all ASEM partners, agree to extend an invitation to a non-ASEM country as well as appropriate international organizations and institutions to take part in a specific event;

the activity must receive SOM's blessing and its results reported to the ASEM SOM.

26. Any proposals for new ASEM initiatives will be presented to all ASEM partners. They may be channelled via the Co-ordinators, who will rapidly disseminate the information to their respective regional partners, and collate comments as necessary. ASEM partners may in addition use the network of contact officers to share new proposals on an informal basis. Proposed initiatives will then be considered and selected by SOM, who will include them as appropriate in the updated work programme to be considered by Foreign Ministers.

27. The results and outputs of all ASEM initiatives will be reported to SOM on a timely basis. SOM shall also be responsible for reviewing the progress achieved under all ASEM initiatives on a regular basis, and for recommending if individual initiatives be continued or terminated. To facilitate this review process, it shall be carried out in such a way as to group activities addressing related issues into thematic clusters.

VI. ASEM PARTICIPATION

28. Building on the conclusions of ASEM 1 in Bangkok and ASEM 2 in London, the following principles should guide future enlargement of the ASEM participation:

the ASEM process, which is open and evolutionary, is intended to reinforce the Asia-Europe partnership,

enlargement should be conducted in progressive stages,

each candidature should be examined on the basis of its own merits and in the light of its potential contribution to the ASEM process,

the two-key approach: a final decision on new participants will be made by consensus among all partners only after a candidate has first got the support of its partners within its region,

any decision regarding the admission of new participants will be taken by the Heads of State and Government on a consensus basis.

VII. REVIEW OF AECF

29. The application of this Framework will be kept under review by SOM and Foreign Ministers on a routine basis, and any necessary adjustments may be recommended by Foreign Ministers for consideration at a future Summit.

ANNEX 3

ACTIVITIES SINCE ASEM 2

I. Ministerial Meetings
1. Foreign Ministers' Meeting in Germany on 28-29 March 1999
2. Economic Ministers' Meeting in Germany on 9-10 October 1999
3. Finance Ministers' Meeting in Germany on 15-16 January 1999
4. Science and Technology Ministers' Meeting in China on 14-15 October 1999

II. Senior Officials' Meetings
Thailand (27-28 October 1998), Finland (2-4 November 1999), Portugal (2-3 May 2000), andKorea (18-20 September 2000)

III. Senior Officials' Meetings on Trade and Investment
Singapore (12-13 February 1999), Belgium (7-8 July 1999) and Korea (12-13 May 2000)

IV. Finance Deputies' Meetings
Austria (18 December 1999), and France (14 September 2000)

V. Other Meetings
1. Asia-Europe Vision Group Meetings
   The United Kingdom (5-6 April 1998), Singapore (2-3 July 1998), Italy (3-4 October 1998), Japan (8-9 January 1999) and Portugal (6-7 February 1999)
2. Asia-Europe Business Forums - Korea (29 September-1 October 1999) and Austria (29-30 September 2000)
3. ASEM Trust Fund Review Meetings - Belgium (8 July 1998), Thailand (20 January 1999), the United Kingdom (22 June 1999), Indonesia (3-4 February 2000) and France (13 September 2000)
4. ASEM Conference: States and Markets in Denmark on 8-10 March 1999
5. ASEM Small and Medium Enterprises' Conference in Italy on 28-30 May 1998
6. Seminar on Industrial Districts and Technology Transfer in Italy on 4-5 October 1999
7. Seminar on Simplification and Harmonization of Customs Procedures in the Philippines on 23-25 February 1999

8. Seminar on Labor Relations in the Netherlands on 26-27 October 1998
9. ASEM Customs Directors-General and Commissioners' Meeting in Belgium on 23 June 1999
10. Customs Working Group on Enforcement - Belgium (5-6 February 1999, and 4-5 February 2000)
11. Customs Working Group on Procedure - The Philippines (26 February 1999) and Belgium (14-15 April 2000)
12. Conference on Trade, Investment and Competition in Austria on 30 September 2000
13. Trade Facilitation Action Plan (TFAP) Meetings on SPS Sector - Thailand (2-5 February 1999), China (23-24 November 1999) and the Netherlands (11-14 September 2000)
14. TFAP Meeting on Standards and conformity - Belgium (30 September-2 October 1998), Korea (10-12 March 1999), Belgium (4-6 October 1999), Thailand (28 February-1 March 2000) and Belgium (2-4 October 2000)
15. TFAP Thematic Meeting on Intellectual Property Rights - France (24-25 June 1999) and Thailand (16-18 March 2000)
16. TFAP Thematic Meeting on Government Procurement in Germany on 14-15 September 1999
17. The Adoption of the Report on ASEM Distribution at SOMTI VI (12-13 May 2000, Seoul)
18. IPAP (Investment Promotion Action Plan) Investment Experts' Group (IEG) Shepherds' Meeting in Thailand on 24 July 1998
19. IPAP Investment Experts Group Meeting - France (23-24 November 1998), Singapore (11 February 1999), Belgium (5-6 July 1999) and Korea (11-12 May 2000)
20. IPAP Decision-Makers' Roundtable in Korea on 1 October 1999
21. Asia-Europe Environmental Technology Center Pilot Phase Guidance Group (PPGG) Meetings - Thailand (25-26 June 1998), Thailand (26-27 November 1998), Thailand (29-30 March 1999), Germany (21-22 June 1999), Japan (9-10 December 1999) and Korea (6-7 July 2000)
22. Asia-Europe Young Leaders Symposia - Austria (25-29 May 1998), Korea (24-28 May 1999) and Ireland (12-16 June 2000)
23. Meeting on the Formation of an ASEM Education Hub Network in France on 25-27 November 1999
24. Preparatory Meeting on ASEM Action on Child Welfare in the Philippines on 15-16 June 1998
25. Child Welfare Experts' Meeting in the United Kingdom on 6-8 October 1998
26. Preparatory Meeting for Child Welfare Meeting of Police and Enforcement Agencies in Manila in March 1999

27. Child Welfare Meeting of Police and Enforcement Agencies in Korea on 4-6 May 2000
28. ASEM Seminar on the Combination of Traditional and Modern Medicine for Public Health Care in Vietnam on 18-19 March 1999
29. ASEM Experts' Meeting on Protection and Promotion of Cultural Heritage in Vietnam on 21-22 January 1999
30. Conference on Cultural Industries and Cultural Development in China on 19-21 May 1999
31. Conference on Asian Crisis, Democracy and Human Rights in Germany on 26-28 March 1999
32. Asia-Europe Workshop on Education in the 21st Century in Luxembourg on 2-3 May 2000
33. Asia-Europe Foundation Board of Governors Meetings - the Netherlands (25 October 1998), China (17-18 May 1999), Denmark (25-26 October 1999), Austria (4-5 May 2000) and Korea (16-17 October 2000).

ANNEX 4

CONTRIBUTORS

ROBERT S. ARENDAL is chief executive, RA Associates, Luxembourg representative to ASEM Vision Group.

JOHN BOYD is vice chairman, ASEM Vision Group, Cambridge, United Kingdom.

KIYOKO IKEGAMI is a member of Resource Mobilisation, International Planned Parenthood Federation, London.

SABINE KUYPERS is Deputy Director of the International Institute for Asian Studies (IIAS), Leiden and Amsterdam.

ANTHONY MURPHY is head of Asia Pacific Trade Policy, Department of Trade and Industry, London.

NURIA OFKEN is a research assistant at the Institute for Social Sciences, Braunscheig, Germany.

NIELS HELVIG PETERSON is Minister of Foreign Affairs of the Kingdom of Denmark and member of the Vision Group of ASEM.

CÉSAR DE PRADO YEPES is a doctoral researcher in the Department of Political and Social Sciences, European University Institute, Florence, Italy.

JÜRGEN RÜLAND is Professor of International Policy and Development Co-operation, Department of Political Science, Faculty of Philosophy, University of Freiburg, Germany.

LEO SCHMIT is a senior researcher at the Projects Division of the Department of Languages and Cultures of Southeast Asia and Oceania at Leiden University.

DALJIT SINGH is a senior research fellow at the Institute of Southeast Asian Studies, Singapore.

NGUYEN SON is senior expert at the Office of the National Committee on Foreign Economic Co-operation, Hanoi, Vietnam.

WIM STOKHOF is director of the International Institute for Asian Studies (IIAS), Leiden and Amsterdam, and secretary of the European Science Foundation Asia Committee as well as member of the Standing Committee of the International Convention of Asian Scholars (ICAS).

PAUL VAN DER VELDE is senior policy advisor at the University van Amsterdam (UvA) and member of the Standing Committee of the International Convention of Asian Scholars (ICAS).

ANNEX 5

ABBREVIATIONS

ADB	Asian Development Bank
AEAF	Asia-Europe Agricultural Forum
AEBF	Asia-Europe Business Forum
AECF	Asia-Europe Cooperation Framework
AEFGC	Asia-Europe Forum of Governors of Cities
AEITTP	Asia-Europe Information Technology and Telecommunications Programme
AFTA	ASEAN Free Trade Area
AMM	ASEAN Annual Ministerial Meeting
APEC	Asia-Pacific Economic Cooperation
ARF	ASEAN Regional Forum
ASEAN	Association of South East Asian Nations
ASEF	Asia-Europe Foundation
ASEM	Asia-Europe Meeting
BISTEC	Bangladesh, India, Sri Lanka and Thailand Economic Cooperation
CBMs	Confidence Building Measures
CEFTA	Central European Free Trade Agreement
DG	Directorate General
EAEC	East Asian Economic Caucus
EC	European Commission
ECAS	Export Credit Agencies
EFTA	European Free Trade Association
EIAS	European Institute for Asian Studies
EMM	Economic Ministers Meeting
EMU	European Economic and Monetary Union
EP	European Parliament
ESF	European Science Foundation
ETSI	European Telecommunications Standardization Institute
EU	European Union
EURATOM	European Atomic Organization
FDIs	Foreign Direct Investments
FPDA	Five Power Defence Arrangements

G-7	Grouping of top 7 industrialized countries
GATS	General Agreement on Trade in Services
GATT	General Agreement on Trade and Tariffs
GDP	Gross Domestic Product
GIP	Global Inventory Project
GIS	Global Information Society
GNP	Gross National Product
IAEA	International Atomic Energy Agency
ICAS	International Convention of Asia Scholars
ICC	International Chamber of Commerce
IEC	International Electro-technical Commission
IEG	Investment Experts Group
IET	Interest Equalization Tax
IFOR	Peace Implementation Force
IIAS	International Institute for Asian Studies
IMF	International Monetary Fund
IPAP	Investment Promotion Action Plan
IOR	Indian Ocean Rim
IOR-ARC	Indian Ocean Rim Association for Regional Cooperation
ISDR	Institute for Security and Development Studies
ISO	International Organization for Standardization
ITU	International Telecommunications Union
KEDO	Korean Peninsula Economic Development Organization
MAI	Multilateral Agreement on Investment
MERCOSUR	Mercado Comun de Sul (Southern Common Market)
MFN	Most Favoured Nation
NAFTA	North American Free Trade Agreement
NATO	North Atlantic Treaty Organization
NICs	Newly Industrialized Countries
NIEs	Newly Industrializing Economies
NPT	Nuclear Non Proliferation Treaty
OAS	Organization of American States
OECD	Organization of Economic Cooperation and Development
OSCE	Organization of Security and Cooperation in Europe
PEARL	Programme for Europe-Asia Research Linkages
PMCs	Post-Ministerial Conferences
PRC	People's Republic of China
SAARC	South Asian Association for Regional Cooperation
SLORC	State Law and Order Restoration Council

SME	Small and Medium size Enterprise
SOMTI	Senior Officers Meeting on Trade and Investment
TAFTA	Transatlantic Free Trade Area
TFAP	Trade Facilitation Action Plan
UHDR	Universal Declaration of Human Rights
UN	United Nations
UNDP	United Nations Development Programme
UNESCO	United Nations Educational, Scientific and Cultural Organization
WIPO	World Intellectual Property Organization
WTO	World Trade Organization

For Product Safety Concerns and Information please contact our EU
representative GPSR@taylorandfrancis.com
Taylor & Francis Verlag GmbH, Kaufingerstraße 24, 80331 München, Germany

www.ingramcontent.com/pod-product-compliance
Lightning Source LLC
Chambersburg PA
CBHW050713280326
41926CB00088B/3005